STUDENT UNIT GUIDE

NEW EDITION

AQA(B) AS Psychology
Unit 1
Introducing Psychology

Julie McLoughlin

PHILIP ALLAN

Philip Allan Updates, an imprint of Hodder Education, an Hachette UK company, Market Place, Deddington, Oxfordshire OX15 OSE

Orders
Bookpoint Ltd, 130 Milton Park, Abingdon, Oxfordshire OX14 4SB
tel: 01235 827827
fax: 01235 400401
e-mail: education@bookpoint.co.uk
Lines are open 9.00 a.m.–5.00 p.m., Monday to Saturday, with a 24-hour message answering service. You can also order through the Philip Allan Updates website: www.philipallan.co.uk

ISBN 978-1-4441-6221-9

First printed 2012
Impression number 5 4 3 2 1
Year 2016 2015 2014 2013 2012

Cover photo: Andreas Karelias/Fotolia

Typeset by Integra, India

Printed in Dubai

Hachette UK's policy is to use papers that are natural, renewable and recyclable products and made from wood grown in sustainable forests. The logging and manufacturing processes are expected to conform to the environmental regulations of the country of origin.

P1993

Contents

Getting the most from this book 4

About this book 5

Content guidance

Approaches

Key approaches in psychology 6

Biopsychology 13

Gender development

Concepts 19

Explaining gender development 21

Research methods

Planning research 29

Experimental methods 31

Non-experimental methods 34

Representing data and descriptive statistics 38

Ethics 42

Questions & Answers

The examination 44

Assessment objectives 46

Q1 Approaches (I) 47

Q2 Approaches (II) 52

Q3 Gender development (I) 57

Q4 Gender development (II) 62

Q5 Research methods (I) 67

Q6 Research methods (II) 73

Knowledge check answers 78

Index 79

7011601086

Getting the most from this book

Examiner tips

Advice from the examiner on key points in the text to help you learn and recall unit content, avoid pitfalls, and polish your exam technique in order to boost your grade.

Knowledge check

Rapid-fire questions throughout the Content guidance section to check your understanding.

Knowledge check answers

1   Turn to the back of the book for the Knowledge check answers.

Summary

Summaries

- Each core topic is rounded off by a bullet-list summary for quick-check reference of what you need to know.

Questions & Answers

Exam-style questions

Examiner comments on the questions
Tips on what you need to do to gain full marks, indicated by the icon ⓔ.

Sample student answers
Practise the questions, then look at the student answers that follow each set of questions.

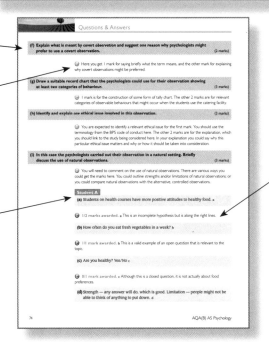

Examiner commentary on sample student answers
Find out how many marks each answer would be awarded in the exam and then read the examiner comments (preceded by the icon ⓔ) following each student answer. Annotations that link back to points made in the student answers show exactly how and where marks are gained or lost.

AQA(B) AS Psychology

About this book

This is a guide to Unit 1 of the AQA(B) AS psychology specification. The guide is intended as a revision *aid* rather than as a textbook. The purpose of the guide is to summarise the content, to explain how the content will be assessed, to look at the type of questions to expect, and to consider specimen answers.

The whole of Unit 1 is compulsory, which means that you must cover everything to be able to answer any questions that appear on the examination paper. In this unit there is no choice of questions. Topic areas covered in the guide are Key Approaches in Psychology and Biopsychology, Gender Development and Research Methods. For each of the topic areas on the specification this guide covers the following:

- the specification content, including exactly what you need to know and learn. The coverage of the content is minimal as you should already have covered the details in your studies. The focus is on key terms and concepts, key theories and studies, and evaluation points. The content here is not the only appropriate material; textbooks will cover the topics in various ways and probably give much more detail and alternative studies.
- two example questions from each of the main topic areas, making a total of six questions. These questions are in the style of AQA(B) questions and similar to those that you might expect to see on real examination papers. To accompany each question there is an analysis of how the question should be tackled and what the examiners are looking for in an answer.
- for each question there are *two* sample answers, A and B. One answer is typical of a borderline grade C/D performance and the other is a high-scoring answer typical of those awarded a grade A. Each answer is followed by a detailed commentary about the marks that have been awarded, drawing attention to any errors or points that are especially creditworthy. There are also suggestions as to how the answers might be improved or elaborated to get extra marks. If you read these sample answers and comments carefully you will learn a lot about what you need to do to present an effective answer in the examination.

How to use this guide

First check your class notes and revision notes against the content presented here to make sure that you have all the *right* material for your revision. Then look at a sample question to see how the examination is structured and what is required. Have a go at the question yourself; then review the sample answers and comments to see where credit can be gained and lost. The sample answers are not intended as model answers but as tools to help you understand what makes a good answer. Finally, you should review your own answer in the light of what you have read and consider how your own response to the question might be improved.

Content guidance

Approaches

Key approaches in psychology

Specification content

The basic assumptions and distinguishing features of the following approaches: biological; behaviourist; social learning theory; cognitive; psychodynamic; and humanistic. The research methods used within each approach. The strengths and limitations of each approach, including the strengths and limitations of associated research methods.

Biological approach

The biological approach focuses on ways in which our biological make-up influences our thoughts and behaviour. In recent years, with the development of more sophisticated scientific techniques and laboratory procedures, the biological approach has become increasingly important in psychology.

The **basic assumptions/features** of the biological approach are as follows:
- Genes influence behaviour. **Genes** are found in the nucleus of every cell and are located on **chromosomes** (bundles of genes) that exist in 23 pairs. This genetic material is passed on from parent to child through sexual reproduction.
- **Biological structures**, such as the brain and nervous system, influence behaviour.
- **Brain chemistry** influences behaviour.
- Behaviour has **evolved**: behaviours that help us survive are more likely to be passed on to future generations than behaviours that do not help us survive.
- There is **behavioural continuity** between species, so it makes sense to study animal species and make a generalisation to human behaviour.

A distinction is made between the genotype, the genetic make-up of individuals, and their phenotype, the actual expression of the genes in an individual. Identical twins have the same genotype because they share 100% of their genes. However, they may not share the same phenotype; one of them may be stronger and more muscular than the other because he works out at the gym. The genotype interacts with environmental influences to produce the phenotype. This can be clearly seen in the genetic condition **phenylketonuria** (PKU). PKU sufferers cannot metabolise phenylalanine, which means that they will have brain damage if they are untreated. However, with a special phenylalanine-free diet, the baby will develop normally. This means that two people with the same PKU genotype could demonstrate quite different phenotypes, one brain damaged and the other quite normal.

Examiner tip
Questions about evolution require you to focus on behaviours such as aggression and the rooting reflex. Be careful not to focus on physiological examples.

Genotype Our genetic make-up.

Phenotype The resulting effect of genes interacting with environment.

Knowledge check 1
According to biopsychologists, what are four main influences on our behaviour?

Research methods

Methods typically used by biological psychologists include surgery (e.g. experiments using animals to see the effects of lesions to the hippocampus on memory); the use of brain-recording techniques and scans, like MRI and PET scans, to observe the activity of living brains in human participants; experiments to test the effects of drugs (e.g. the effects of medication on children with autism); analysis of case studies of individuals who have suffered some kind of brain damage to see how their behaviour has been affected; twin studies to see how alike identical and non-identical twins are for various characteristics.

Autism A developmental disorder characterised by poor communication and lack of interest in other people.

Strengths of the biological approach

- The methods are highly scientific.
- Knowing how biology is involved in psychological disorders enables researchers to find suitable treatments.

Limitations of the biological approach

- Extreme biological explanations undervalue the possible influences of social factors and environment.
- Explaining complex behaviours at the levels of cells and chemicals is an over-simplification. This is known as reductionism.
- It seems to suggest that the mind and the brain are the same thing.
- It suggests that people do not have free will to decide how to behave. This is known as biological determinism.
- There are ethical implications. For example, if behaviour such as criminality is found to be genetic, what should we do about it?
- There are problems generalising findings from animal research to humans.

Knowledge check 2

What is meant by biological determinism?

Behaviourist approach

Behaviourism developed in the USA in the early twentieth century and was for a long time the dominant approach in psychology. Behaviourists carried out highly controlled experiments to investigate how behaviour is learned. The **basic assumptions/ features** of the behaviourist approach are as follows:

- All behaviour is **learned** through association and can be understood in terms of stimulus–response (SR) links.
- Behaviour depends on **consequences**. If a behaviour has a pleasant consequence then it is likely to be repeated. If it has an unpleasant consequence then it is not likely to be repeated.
- Psychology should be **scientific** and **objective**. Psychologists should only study observable behaviour; mental processes like memory and attention are not appropriate subject matter for psychologists.
- It is sensible to generalise from animal research to human behaviour.

Examiner tip

Do not confuse traditional behaviourism (learning by association) with social learning theory (learning by observation).

Research methods

Behaviourist psychologists normally conduct controlled laboratory experiments, often using animals as subjects.

Classical conditioning

Classical conditioning theory was used by the behaviourists to explain simple learned associations. Pavlov studied salivation in dogs. He found that by pairing food with the sound of a bell, a dog learned to associate the food and bell. After a number of pairings, the bell alone would produce salivation in the dog. The dog had been conditioned to respond to a previously neutral stimulus. Pavlov termed this process 'classical conditioning' and it is shown in the table below, which charts the progression from unconditioned stimulus to conditioned response. Classical conditioning is a basic form of learning that can only be applied to involuntary reflex behaviours such as salivation, eye blinking and fear.

Examiner tip
Practise drawing classical
conditioning stage
diagrams to explain
different examples of
classically conditioned
behaviours, e.g. fear of
flying or school phobia.

Stages involved in classical conditioning

Stage 1	Food (UCS)	elicits	salivation (UCR)
Stage 2	Food (UCS) + bell (CS)	elicits	salivation (UCR)
Stage 3	Bell (CS)	elicits	salivation (CR)

UCS = unconditioned stimulus; CS = conditioned stimulus; UCR = unconditioned response; CR = conditioned response

Classical conditioning was demonstrated in humans by Watson and Raynor (1920), who conditioned a fear of white furry things in a baby, Little Albert, by repeatedly making a loud noise every time he played with his pet white rat.

Knowledge check 3
What sorts of behaviours
can be learned through
classical conditioning?

The following key concepts are associated with classical conditioning:
- **generalisation** — producing the conditioned response to a stimulus that is similar to the original conditioned stimulus
- **discrimination** — not responding to a stimulus that is different from the original conditioned stimulus
- **extinction** — a conditioned response dies out after repeated presentation of the conditioned stimulus without the unconditioned stimulus

Operant conditioning

Operant conditioning theory was used by the behaviourists to explain how voluntary behaviours are learned. Skinner (1953) carried out experiments with rats using a Skinner Box. He found that rats would quickly learn to associate pressing a bar with food. Skinner described the food as reinforcement since it strengthened the learned behaviour, making it more likely to occur. The different types of reinforcement are as follows:

Examiner tip
Do not confuse negative
reinforcement and
punishment. Negative
reinforcement is avoidance
learning: performing
the behaviour (doing
homework) avoids the
consequence (detention);
punishment: performing
the behaviour leads to the
consequence (detention).

- **positive reinforcement** — a pleasant stimulus is received after a behaviour is performed
- **negative reinforcement** — a behaviour is performed to avoid an unpleasant stimulus (avoidance learning)
- **punishment**: an unpleasant stimulus is received after a behaviour is performed
- **primary reinforcement** — something that is in itself rewarding, e.g. sweets
- **secondary reinforcement** — something that is not in itself rewarding but can be exchanged for something that is, e.g. tokens, money

Strengths of the behaviourist approach

- It uses highly controlled scientific methods.
- It enables the prediction of behaviour.
- Many therapies have been derived from behaviourist theory, e.g. token economy systems where people in institutions are given tokens for good behaviour. These tokens can later be exchanged for treats.

Strengths of the behaviourist approach

- It assumes that biological factors have little influence on behaviour.
- It neglects mental processes and emotions.
- Behaviour is seen as being determined by the environment, suggesting there is no free will. This is known as environmental determinism.
- It may not be sensible to generalise from animal research to human behaviour.
- Seeing all behaviour in terms of simple SR links is an oversimplification.

Knowledge check 4

Why is operant conditioning able to explain a wider range of learned behaviours than classical conditioning?

Social learning theory

Social learning theory was developed in the 1960s to take account of the importance of social factors and mental processes in human learning. Social learning theorists focused on observational learning in humans. The **basic assumptions/features** of social learning theory are as follows:

- Behaviour is learned through **observation** and **imitation**.
- **Modelling** is performing a behaviour demonstrated by a model, a person with whom we identify.
- **Identification** with someone involves a desire to be like them and therefore leads to a desire to imitate them.
- Reinforcement can be vicarious — we can learn through observation of the consequences for others of their actions.
- **Mediating cognitive factors** (mental processes like memory and thinking) occur between stimulus and response; we do not observe and automatically imitate but think about several factors before we imitate. For example, we would think about whether we are physically able to carry out the action we have observed, and whether we want to or not. We are more likely to produce modelling behaviour if the model is perceived to be attractive, of high status and similar to ourselves. Also, we are more likely to show modelling behaviour if the behaviour is seen to be appropriate and if the model is seen to be rewarded.

Vicarious reinforcement Indirect reinforcement through observation of the consequences of other people's actions.

Knowledge check 5

What do social learning theorists mean by mediating cognitive factors?

Research methods

Social learning theorists usually carry out experiments with human participants, with observational techniques used to gather data. In a sequence of studies, Bandura, Ross and Ross (1960s) showed children an adult (a model) behaving aggressively towards an inflatable Bobo doll. It was found that the children would model the behaviour, although the likelihood of modelling occurring depended on factors such as the characteristics of the model and whether he/she was seen to be rewarded or punished.

Examiner tip

Earn evaluation marks in 10-mark questions by noting an important difference between traditional behaviourism and social learning theory: social learning theory takes account of the role of thinking processes (mediating cognitive factors) in learning; behaviourism does not.

Strengths of social learning theory

- It considers the role of cognitive factors in learning.
- It explains the learning of complex human behaviours such as aggression.

Limitations of social learning theory

- The Bobo doll experiment is highly artificial. It lacks ecological validity.
- Not all behaviours are learned by observation and can be readily copied; some takes years of practice while others are classically or operantly conditioned.

Knowledge check 6

What do cognitive psychologists mean by the term *model*?

Cognitive approach

The cognitive approach became popular in the 1950s and 1960s with the development of computers. Cognitive psychologists focus on internal mental processing and the influence of thought on behaviour. The **basic assumptions/features** of the cognitive approach are as follows:

- **Internal mental processes**, like memory and perception, can be studied scientifically.
- Humans **actively** process information.
- Human information processing is similar to the way a **computer** processes information, proceeding through a sequence of stages from **input** to **output**.
- Theoretical **models** (structured theories usually represented as flow charts) can be used to explain cognitive processes.

Examiner tip

Be clear about the computer analogy. Cognitive psychologists assume human **processing** is similar to computer **processing**. They do not say humans are like computers.

One model used to explain cognitive processes is the multi-store model of memory (Atkinson and Shiffrin 1968). The model presents memory as a stage-based sequence in the form of a flow chart. This is typical of how cognitive psychologists use models to explain cognitive processes.

Research methods

Methods typically used by cognitive psychologists include controlled laboratory experiments investigating mental processes in human participants; case studies of single individuals who have a cognitive impairment (e.g. a memory disorder or language problem); computer modelling of human processes (e.g. a computer face-recognition programme); use of scans to enable investigation of the neurological activity when various cognitive processes are taking place.

A typical study of internal mental processing is a memory experiment where participants hear a list of unconnected words and then have to recall them in any order. It is usually found that participants recall the first and last words on the list, but tend to recall few from the middle. This is known as the primacy–recency effect. These findings have been used to understand the way that memory works; it is suggested that the first words on the list have been rehearsed and therefore are recalled from long-term memory, whereas the last words on the list are recalled from short-term memory.

Knowledge check 7

Identify four research methods used by cognitive psychologists.

Strengths of the cognitive approach

- It considers the role of thinking in behaviour.
- Cognitive models help to explain complex thinking processes by separating a complex process into its separate components.
- It focuses on investigations using human participants.
- It uses highly controlled scientific methods.
- Successful therapies have been developed using cognitive principles, e.g. cognitive behaviour therapy for depression, where the therapist tries to get the depressed person to have more positive thoughts.

Limitations of the cognitive approach

- Traditional cognitive research relies on inference; we can only guess about what mental processes are taking place on the basis of the results of an experiment.
- The cognitive approach says little about the initial causes of behaviour.
- It takes a mechanistic view, likening human processing to the workings of a machine.
- Cognitive experiments tend to be highly artificial, lacking in ecological validity.

Psychodynamic approach

The psychodynamic approach was initiated by Freud at the beginning of the twentieth century. Freud emphasised the **role of the unconscious**, suggesting that we are consciously aware of only a small proportion of our thought, and that our unconscious wishes and fears influence our conscious behaviour and our personality. The **basic assumptions/features** of the psychodynamic approach are as follows:

- **Unconscious** mental processes motivate our behaviour.
- Personality has three parts: the **id**, which is unreasonably demanding and self-serving, like a little child who demands instant satisfaction; the **superego**, which is the over-demanding, strict and punishing internal parent or conscience that makes us feel guilty; the **ego**, which is the conscious self resulting from the competing demands of the id and the superego.
- **Early childhood experiences** influence adult behaviour and personality. Problems like anxiety in adult life are often due to unpleasant early experiences of which we are not consciously aware.
- Development takes place in **psychosexual stages**. At each stage the child derives satisfaction from a different area of the body, for example, in the oral stage the child enjoys oral stimulation from breast or bottle feeding. At each stage there is a conflict to be resolved; if this conflict is not satisfactorily resolved, then the child will become fixated at that stage. As an example, the conflict in the oral stage revolves around weaning. If there are problems at the weaning stage then the person will have an oral fixation, engaging in oral behaviours such as nail-biting in adulthood.
- **Defence mechanisms** are unconscious processes that act to protect the conscious self from unpleasant events in the world or unpleasant thoughts about the self. Examples include: denial — refusing to believe that an unpleasant event is happening; repression — motivated forgetting.

Ecological validity The extent to which a behaviour has been measured in circumstances similar to the way in which that behaviour occurs in everyday life.

Examiner tip
Check your spellings — students often confuse 'conscience' and 'conscious'. Making mistakes here can change the meaning of your answer.

Fixation Becoming stuck at a particular psychosexual stage of development because a childhood conflict has not been satisfactorily resolved. This will affect our adult behaviour.

Examiner tip

Be able to describe 'defence mechanisms' in general terms and to explain specific defence mechanisms such as repression and denial. Also be able to give examples of how defence mechanisms might be involved in coping with everyday situations such as failing a driving test.

Knowledge check 8

What is it that motivates all our behaviour, according to Freud?

Examiner tip

Most students are overly critical of psychodynamic theory and Freud. In a discussion question, remember to present a balanced evaluation with some positive points as well as criticisms.

Examiner tip

Be clear about the concept of free will. Free will, the ability to choose how to behave, is not the same as 'being able to do whatever you like'.

- Psychological problems can be treated through accessing the unconscious using methods involved in the Freudian therapy known as **psychoanalysis**, such as free association or analysis of dreams.

Research methods

The main method used in the psychodynamic approach is the case study. This is because most research in this area has been carried out with individual cases of people who consulted Freud and other psychoanalysts because they were suffering from neurotic or anxiety disorders. One such case is Little Hans, a young boy who was suffering from a phobia of horses. Freud suggested that Little Hans was not really afraid of horses but in fact was afraid of his father (see p. 28).

Strengths of the psychodynamic approach

- Freud recognised the importance of childhood experiences for later life.
- The idea of unconscious mental activity is appealing.
- Defence mechanisms offer plausible explanations for everyday behaviour and experiences.
- Psychoanalysis has had some reported success and has led to the development of other psychological therapies.

Limitations of the psychodynamic approach

- It is often accused of being male-oriented.
- It over-emphasises the sexual instinct as a motivating factor, even suggesting that it influences childhood behaviour.
- The theories and concepts are not based on scientific evidence.
- The unconscious cannot be verified or tested. As such, the theory is unfalsifiable.
- Freud is often accused of fitting his cases to his already existing theory.
- It is inappropriate to base a theory of all human behaviour on just a few case studies.
- It focuses on the past, stressing the negative effects of past experiences.

Humanistic approach

The humanistic approach became popular in the 1960s as part of a rejection of the mechanistic science of the behaviourists and the pessimism of psychoanalysis. Humanistic psychologists rejected the scientific approach in psychology because they believed that the focus should be on the individual and therefore it is not sensible to make generalisations. The approach is sometimes described as being 'anti-science'. The **basic assumptions/features** of the humanistic approach are as follows:

- People have the **free will** to determine their own destiny. This is in contrast to the determinism of the biological and behaviourist approaches.
- The emphasis is on the **self**. Carl Rogers felt that psychological problems were due to differences between the perceived self and the ideal self. He referred to this difference as incongruence. Rogers suggested that incongruence between the perceived and ideal self are due to other people, usually parents, imposing

conditions of worth. In other words, loving and accepting their children only if they fulfil certain conditions. To counter this, Rogers suggested that people need unconditional positive regard — to be loved and accepted for what they are.

- All people have a unique experience of the world (their own **phenomenology**). Everyone is essentially good and in the right conditions can grow and self-actualise (reach their full potential).
- Behaviour is motivated by a **hierarchy of needs** with basic survival needs at the bottom and the need to self-actualise (be fulfilled) at the top.
- Therapy should be **client-centred**. It should also be **holistic** (considering all aspects of a person), **empathic** (appreciating the client's feelings) and genuine.

Research methods

Humanistic psychologists study individuals using the case study method or study people interacting in group therapy sessions. One of the few attempts at objective measurement is a test known as the Q-sort, where people have to sort cards into piles according to whether they think the description on the card is like them or not. The Q-sort is used to test a person's self-perception.

Strengths of the humanistic approach

- It offers a more optimistic and forward-looking view of human nature than the psychodynamic approach.
- It credits the person as being responsible for their own behaviour.
- Client-centred therapy is effective for minor problems and has led to the growth of counselling.

Limitations of the humanistic approach

- Perhaps it is unrealistically optimistic; maybe some people can never self-actualise.
- The concepts of self and self-actualisation may not apply in other cultures, for example, collectivist cultures such as China.
- It is unscientific, rejecting scientific methods and principles. This means that humanistic ideas and concepts cannot be properly investigated.
- The focus on the individual means that generalisations cannot be made about all human behaviour.

Biopsychology

Specification content

Neurons and synaptic transmission. The divisions of the nervous system. Localisation of function in the brain. Methods used to identify areas of cortical specialisation. Actions of the sympathetic and parasympathetic divisions of the autonomic nervous system.

Conditions of worth Where people are loved and accepted only if they fulfil certain conditions.

Self-actualisation Realisation of one's full potential.

Knowledge check 9

Give an example of how a parent might place conditions of worth on his or her child.

Examiner tip

Client-centred therapy is non-directive — clients find their own solutions to their problems and are not told what to do by the therapist. Contrast this type of therapy with Freudian therapy, which is more directive.

Neurons and synaptic transmission

Neurons are nerve cells. The human nervous system has around 100 billion neurons. Neurons send and receive electrical information, or nerve impulses, either from other neurons, or other cells (e.g. muscle cells, heart cells).

- **Sensory neurons** carry information from the senses to the central nervous system.
- **Motor neurons** transmit messages from the central nervous system to the muscles.
- **Interneurons** (connector neurons) connect neurons to other neurons. Approximately 95% of these are in the brain.

Examiner tip

Practise labelling a diagram of a neuron, as you might be asked to do this in the examination. Make sure you can describe the function/purpose of each labelled part.

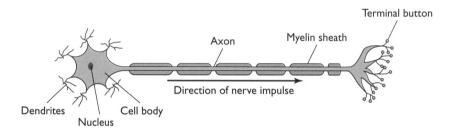

Figure 1 A motor neuron

A neuron (see Figure 1) has a **cell body**, an **axon** and branch-like **dendrites**. The cell body has a nucleus containing our **DNA** or genetic material. Within the cell, information travels by means of electrical impulses. The axon extends from the cell body. Axons are covered with a fatty **myelin sheath**, which insulates the axon and speeds up transmission of electrical impulses along it. The **terminal button** at the end of the axon houses **vesicles** (tiny sacs) containing chemicals known as **neurotransmitters**. Adjacent neurons do not actually touch one another, between them is a gap known as the **synapse** or synaptic cleft. When an electrical impulse travels to the end of the axon, the vesicles release their neurotransmitter across the synapse. This chemical then locks into special receptor sites on the dendrite of the adjacent neuron. From there the electrical nerve impulse is transmitted in the same way through the next neuron. Some neurotransmitters increase the rate of firing between neurons whilst others decrease the rate of firing. The movement of an electrical impulse along the axon is called an **action potential.** This happens when a chemical process alters the electric charge, both inside and outside of the neuron.

Knowledge check 10

Name and describe three types of neurons.

Neurotransmitters

Neurotransmitters are brain chemicals that affect cognitive processes and behaviour.

- **Acetylcholine (ACH)** is found at synapses between motor neurons and muscle cells and is responsible for movement.
- **Dopamine** affects arousal, pleasure and voluntary movement. Too much dopamine is thought to be responsible for schizophrenia.
- **Serotonin** governs sleep, aggression and mood. Low levels of serotonin are associated with depression.

Neurotransmitters

Brain chemicals that are used to pass messages between neurons.

Divisions of the nervous system

The human nervous system is divided into the central nervous system and the peripheral nervous system, as shown in Figure 2.

The central nervous system is made up of the brain and spinal cord. The spinal cord receives and passes messages to and from the brain, and connects to nerves in the peripheral nervous system.

The **peripheral nervous system** consists of neurons that send information to and from the central nervous system. It is divided into the somatic and autonomic nervous systems.

The **somatic nervous system** transmits information received by the senses to the central nervous system and sends messages from the central nervous system to the muscles.

The **autonomic nervous system** is divided into the sympathetic and parasympathetic sections. The autonomic nervous system links the central nervous system to internal organs and controls basic functions such as breathing and digestion. It cannot be controlled voluntarily.

Central nervous system The brain and spinal cord.

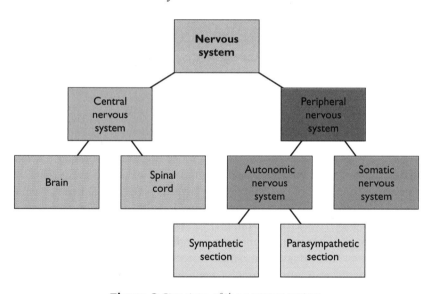

Figure 2 Structure of the nervous system

Knowledge check 11

What is the function of the autonomic nervous system? What are its two sub-divisions?

Localisation of function

The notion that different areas of the brain have different functions is known as localisation of function. The human brain has two hemispheres responsible for higher cognitive functions, such as thinking and remembering. They are joined by the **corpus callosum**, a set of nerve fibres allowing information to be transferred between the two hemispheres. The right hemisphere is mostly responsible for the left side of the body, and the left hemisphere for the right side of the body. Lateralisation of function refers to the way that the two hemispheres have different functions (also referred to as hemispheric specialisation). In right-handed people the left side of the brain is most important for language function, logic and analysis and the right side is most important for non-linguistic processing (e.g. music and emotion). The opposite is true for people who are left-handed.

Different functions are located in different areas of the cortex:
- Movement is located in the motor cortex to the rear of the frontal lobe.
- Sensory processing (touch) is located in the somatosensory cortex in the parietal lobe, to the rear of the motor cortex.
- Vision is located in the visual cortex in the occipital lobe at the rear of the cortex.
- Auditory (sound) processing is located in the left temporal lobe.

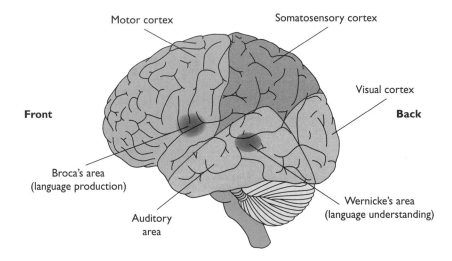

Figure 3 Different areas of the brain

Examiner tip

Practise labelling a diagram of the areas of the brain, as you might be asked to do this in the examination. Make sure you can describe the function/ purpose of each area.

Localisation of language

Broca's area, to the left of the frontal lobe, governs speech production. Damage to Broca's area causes speech to be slow and laborious. **Wernicke's area**, in the left temporal lobe, governs the understanding of speech. Damage to this area causes comprehension problems and the person's speech is fluent but meaningless. Studies using brain scans have shown that either Broca's area or Wernicke's area is active when people perform different types of language task. For example, listening to nouns involves Wernicke's area, and thinking of verbs to go in a phrase uses Broca's area (Peterson et al. 1988).

Evaluation

Knowledge check 12

Which areas of the brain are responsible for
(i) language production and (ii) language comprehension?

- Although some functions can be located in certain areas of the brain, most functions involve many inter-connected areas of the brain. In other words, brain function is **holistic**.
- People with brain damage to a specific area (e.g. after a stroke) often recover function over time because another area of the brain takes over. This is referred to as **brain plasticity**.

AQA(B) AS Psychology

Methods used to identify cortical specialisation

Post-mortem examinations

A post-mortem examination involves surgical dissection of the brain of a person who has died. Paul Broca (1824–80) used post-mortem examinations in an attempt to link visible signs of brain damage with how the person had behaved when they were alive. This is how he discovered that language function was located on the left side of the brain in the area now known as Broca's area. While they provide an interesting insight into rare cases of brain-damaged individuals, post-mortems cannot tell us anything about the functioning of a living brain. It is also possible that the process of death may have changed the brain in some way.

Post-mortem Surgical dissection after death.

Electroencephalograms (EEGs)

Electroencephalograms record the electrical activity of areas of the brain using electrodes that are placed on the head. Brain wave patterns coming from the activity of lots of neurons can be seen on a screen. EEGs have been used to study normal brain activity, for example, the different patterns of activity in the sleeping and waking brain, and brain activity in cases of conditions such as epilepsy. They give an overall picture of brain activity and have become more sophisticated, with computers used to analyse recordings from large numbers of electrodes. While easy to use and not harmful, they tend to give a fairly generalised measure and are therefore not very useful in identifying specific areas of cortical specialisation.

Electroencephalogram (EEG) Surface electrodes used to record brain activity.

Knowledge check 13

What three methods are used to identify areas of cortical specialisation?

Scans

Positron-emission tomography (PET) involves the injection of a radioactive chemical into the bloodstream. The head is then scanned to see the amount of radioactivity coming from different parts of the brain. The amount of radioactivity increases with increased blood flow, indicating which areas of the brain are most active. PET scans can be used to see which parts of the brain are involved in different mental tasks, such as reading. In magnetic resonance imaging (MRI) strong magnetic fields and radio waves produce multiple images that combine to give a detailed image of the structure of the brain. Computerised axial tomography (CAT) involves taking multiple X-rays from different positions around the head. These are combined on a computer to produce cross-sectional images of the brain. Scanning techniques have greatly advanced understanding of brain function, can be used with live human brains, and are more accurate and less invasive than many other methods.

Examiner tip

Be able to discuss strengths and limitations of these methods. The focus of your discussion should be on how well the method(s) enable us to study areas of cortical specialisation (how much they tell us about which parts of the brain perform which functions).

Autonomic nervous system

The autonomic nervous system connects the central nervous system with smooth muscled organs and glands and is part of the **peripheral nervous system**. The functions of the autonomic nervous system (e.g. increased heart rate) are not normally under conscious control. The autonomic nervous system is divided into the sympathetic and parasympathetic sections. The **sympathetic section** prepares the body for action in an emergency or exciting situation. The **parasympathetic section** has the opposite effect, bringing the body back to its normal state. Imagine

that you are walking alone down a dark lane at night and you hear a noise. The action of the sympathetic section of the autonomic nervous system prepares you for 'fight or flight'. When the danger has passed, the action of the parasympathetic section restores your body functions back to their normal state of 'rest and digest'.

Examiner tip

Learn the sympathetic and parasympathetic effects. Applied questions often give examples of people in dangerous or arousing situations and ask you to link their bodily responses to the activity of the autonomic nervous system.

Effects of the sympathetic and parasympathetic sections of the autonomic nervous system

Sympathetic action	Parasympathetic action
Heart rate increases	Heart rate decreases
Pupil dilates	Pupil constricts
Intestine/gut action slows	Intestine/gut action restored
Salivation stops (mouth dries)	Salivation restored

Endocrine system: the adrenal glands

Endocrine system System of glands that secrete chemicals known as hormones into the bloodstream.

Glands in the endocrine system secrete **hormones** into the bloodstream. These are chemical messengers that affect body organs. The **pituitary gland** is the 'master gland'; the hormones it releases regulate the activity of other glands. The pituitary gland is controlled by the **hypothalamus** in the brain.

Role of the adrenal glands in stress

The adrenal gland is involved in stress in two separate ways:

- The brain stimulates the sympathetic nervous system, which in turn stimulates the adrenal gland to release adrenalin. This causes the 'adrenalin rush' that we experience at times of stress or anxiety (e.g. when tripping on the stairs).
- The hypothalamus stimulates the pituitary gland, which instructs the adrenal gland to release the hormone cortisol. Cortisol activates the release of glucose into the bloodstream for energy.

Knowledge check 14

Hormones are chemical messengers that travel in the bloodstream. What is the name of the chemical messengers that communicate between neurons in the brain?

Knowledge check 15

Which hormone is produced by the adrenal gland and what is the main function of this hormone?

Glands of the endocrine system and their main functions

Gland	Function
Pituitary gland	Master gland, controls other glands
Thyroid gland	Produces thyroxin, for regulation of growth and metabolism
Adrenal gland	Produces adrenalin, responsible for the fight or flight reaction
Ovaries	Produce oestrogen and progesterone, responsible for female sexual behaviour
Testes	Produce testosterone, responsible for male sexual behaviour

- Biopsychologists study the influence of genes, biological structures (brain, nervous system), neurotransmitters and hormones. They assume that behaviour has evolved. Methods: experiments, case studies, twin studies, specialist techniques, for example scans.

- Behaviourists assume behaviour is learnt through association. Pavlov studied classical conditioning in dogs conditioned to salivate (CR) to the sound of a bell (CS) that had been paired with food (UCS). Skinner studied operant conditioning in rats conditioned to bar-press when reinforced with food. Method: controlled animal experiments.

- Social learning theorists study observational learning. They stress the role of mediating cognitive factors (thinking) in learning. The Bobo doll experiment showed how children would imitate aggressive behaviour. Method: experiments with observation.

- Cognitive psychologists study internal mental processes. They propose theoretical models (e.g. multi-store model), comparing human processing to the processing of a computer. Method: controlled laboratory experiments, computer modelling, case studies.

- Psychodynamic psychologists believe unconscious processes influence behaviour. They emphasise the importance of early experience, especially the psychosexual stages. They believe personality has three parts (id, ego, superego). Methods: case studies, psychoanalysis (therapy).

- Humanistic psychologists focus on self-actualisation and how conditions of worth affect the self. They believe we have free will. Methods: case studies, client-centred therapy.

- Biopsychology in detail:
  - Neurons: motor (brain to muscles), sensory (senses to brain), inter (in the brain)
  - Synaptic transmission: messages between neurons by means of neurotransmitter
  - Divisions of the nervous system: CNS (central), PNS (peripheral), SNS (somatic — senses/muscles), ANS (autonomic = automatic)
  - The ANS has two sections: sympathetic (increases arousal — fight or flight); parasympathetic (restores resting state — rest and digest)
  - Adrenal glands in the endocrine system secrete adrenalin, which increases arousal in times of stress
  - Different areas of the brain are specialised for motor (movement), somatosensory (touch), visual (vision), auditory (hearing) functions. Language areas: Broca's: production; Wernicke's: comprehension
  - Cortical specialisation is studied using post-mortems, EEGs, PET and other scans

Gender development

Concepts

Specification content

Sex and gender: androgyny; sex-role stereotypes; cultural variations in gender-related behaviour; nature and nurture.

Sex and gender

Sex is a biological term referring to our status as either male or female. It is determined by chromosomes, hormones and anatomical differences.

Gender is a psychosocial term referring to the roles, attitudes and behaviours associated with being either male or female. These differ according to the society in which we live, making gender a **social construction**.

What is the difference between sex and gender?

Androgyny Possessing a balance of male and female characteristics.

Related terms include **masculine** and **feminine.** Masculine behaviours, roles and attitudes are those thought to be appropriate for males. Feminine behaviours, roles and attitudes are those thought to be appropriate for females.

Androgyny is a term meaning the possession of both masculine and feminine characteristics. It has been proposed that androgynous people are more psychologically healthy than people who are either strongly masculine or strongly feminine.

Bem's sex-role inventory (BSRI) (1974) measures androgyny. To complete the BSRI, respondents have to rate themselves on a 7-point scale for a list of traits such as warm, gentle, forceful and aggressive. After completing the questionnaire, an overall masculinity score and an overall femininity score can be calculated. This allows the respondent to plot themselves on the two dimensions.

Examiner tip

Make sure you can describe how psychologists such as Bem have studied androgyny. There are on-line versions of the BSRI for you to try so you can see for yourself how androgyny scales work.

Evaluation

- Other researchers argue that a high masculinity score is important for psychological well-being rather than a mixture of masculine and feminine traits.
- Reducing complicated concepts to a single score based on a list of traits is an oversimplification. More recently, researchers have measured other aspects of gender, like hobbies and abilities, rather than just personality characteristics.
- The BSRI was developed using American students' views of what was desirable in men and women in the 1970s.
- The BSRI produces similar results if repeated with the same sample, so it is reliable.

Sex-role or gender stereotypes

A sex-role stereotype or gender stereotype is a fixed belief about what we expect of males and females. It can include beliefs about behaviours, attitudes and traits. For example, according to traditional gender stereotypes, males are expected to be good at practical things like putting up shelves, to enjoy sport and be brave. In contrast, females are expected to be good at looking after children, to enjoy shopping and be gentle.

Study

Examiner tip

You could be asked to describe how psychologists have studied sex-role stereotyping. You might also be asked to discuss (evaluate) these studies. Also, be able to give everyday examples of sex-role stereotyping e.g. expecting lorry drivers to be male; expecting women to be emotional.

Seavey, Katz and Zalk (1975) studied how adults reacted to a baby that they thought was either male or female. Adult participants were left with a 3-month-old baby dressed in a yellow baby outfit for 3 minutes. Available toys included a ball, a rag doll and a plastic ring. When told the child was female, participants tended to give the child the doll, but when told the baby was male, they tended to give the baby the plastic ring. The researchers concluded that adults behave differently towards babies according to what sex they think the babies are. This is an example of what is known as a 'Baby X' study. In general, experiments like this show that how a baby is labelled, as either male or female, affects the way the infant is treated and played with.

Study

Urberg (1982) investigated children's gender stereotypes. Children aged three, five and seven years heard stories in which characters whose sex was unspecified showed traits such as gentleness or bravery. After listening to the story, the children were then asked who showed the trait in the story — a woman, a man, or neither. They found that all children answered according to gender stereotypes, showing that children have clear beliefs about the characteristics and behaviours typical of males and females.

Cultural variations in gender-related behaviour

Mead (1935) studied differences in gender roles in three different societies in New Guinea. She found that there were cultural differences in gender-related behaviour. Males and females in the Arapesh society were gentle and cooperative, behaving in a typically feminine way. Males and females in the Mundugamor society behaved in a typically male, aggressive way. Males and females in the Tchambuli society had distinct gender roles that were the opposite of traditional Western sex roles. This is an example of a cross-cultural study, comparing the behaviours and attitudes shown in different cultures. Any differences found to exist between cultures are then assumed to be due to differences in socialisation and experience.

Evaluation

- Mead's methods have been criticised for being unscientific.
- Mead may have been biased. She expected to find cultural differences and this expectation perhaps affected her observations.
- Mead later changed her ideas about the extent to which culture influences gender and suggested that women were 'naturally' better at caring for children than men.
- Mead has been accused of exaggerating cultural differences in gender-related behaviour.
- The general notion of cultural differences in gender-related behaviour may be correct; Wade and Tavris (1998) reported cultural differences: for example, the status of women is relatively high in Scandinavian countries and very low in Bangladesh.

Examiner tip
Mead's study can also be used as evidence in favour of the social learning explanation of gender.

Nature and nurture

The nature–nurture debate is concerned with the relative importance of the influences of biology and the environment on our behaviour. According to the **nature** view, gender is predominantly the result of biological factors such as genes and hormones. According to the **nurture** view, gender is predominantly the result of environmental factors such as family, education and life experiences. The mid-point in the debate would be the **interactionist** view that both nature and nurture contribute to gender. In any discussion of the nature–nurture debate in relation to gender, it is important to refer to explanations of gender, in particular, the explanations offered by biological and social learning theory.

Knowledge check 17
How does the nature–nurture debate relate to gender?

Explaining gender development

Specification content

Biological explanations: typical and atypical sex chromosomes; androgens and oestrogens. Social learning theory: reinforcement; modelling; imitation and identification. Cognitive approach: Kohlberg's cognitive developmental theory including gender identity, stability

and constancy; gender schema theory. Psychodynamic approach: Freud's psychoanalytic theory; Oedipus complex; Electra complex; identification.

Biological explanations of gender

Biological psychologists explain gender in terms of:

- chromosomes
- brain structure
- hormones

Typical sex chromosome patterns

Biological sex is determined by the combination of chromosomes for the 23rd chromosome pair.

For males, the typical sex chromosome pattern is XY. For females, the typical sex chromosome pattern is XX.

Atypical sex chromosome patterns

A condition known as **Klinefelter's syndrome** involves the presence of an extra X chromosome, giving a combination of XXY. Klinefelter's syndrome occurs in between one in 500 and one in 1000 males. People with Klinefelter's syndrome are biological males. They tend to behave passively in relation to most males, have poor language skills and are infertile. Physically tall, their legs are long in relation to the torso.

The condition **Turner's syndrome** occurs in females who have only one X chromosome, resulting in the combination XO. Turner's syndrome affects one in 2500 females. People with Turner's syndrome are biological females. They usually have good verbal ability and poor visual–spatial ability. They have no functioning ovaries and usually have a short and squat physique.

Studying the psychological effects of atypical sex chromosome patterns allows us to make inferences about the effects of male and female chromosomes on psychological functioning in people with typical sex chromosome combinations.

Study

The case of the Batista boys shows how chromosomal constitution can be more important for gender identity than how we are raised. Imperato-McGinley (1979) studied boys in a family with a genetic abnormality. The boys appeared female at birth and were brought up as females. However, because of a genetic mutation, they changed into boys at puberty. Their chromosome pattern was always XY (that of a normal male). Despite having been treated for years as girls, these boys adjusted well to their male identity showing how biology can override socialisation.

Study

The case of Bruce Reimer (Money and Ehrhardt 1972) showed how socialisation cannot overcome biology. Bruce lost his penis in a routine operation when he was a baby. His parents were advised to bring him up as a girl. Bruce had gender

Examiner tip

Questions on Klinefelter's syndrome and Turner's syndrome may ask about the physical *or* psychological characteristics associated with the syndrome. Make sure you are clear which characteristics are physical and which are psychological.

Knowledge check 18

Why do psychologists study people with atypical sex chromosome patterns?

re-assignment surgery and was given the female hormone oestrogen at puberty. Despite years of being socialised as a female, Bruce eventually rejected the female role and reverted to being male. He stopped the oestrogen treatment and later had further surgery to restore his male appearance. The case suggests that biological influences (XY chromosomes) are more important than socialisation.

Evaluation

- Both cases are unusual and may not therefore tell us much about normal gender development.

Examiner tip
The cases of the Batista boys and Bruce Reimer can be used as evidence *for* the biological explanation of gender and *against* the social learning explanation of gender.

Brain structure

Perhaps brain differences between males and females affect gender-related behaviour. Gorski et al. (1978) discovered that a region of the hypothalamus known as the sexually dimorphic nucleus is larger in male rats than in female rats. This difference is thought to be due to the action of the male hormone testosterone.

Sexually dimorphic nucleus An area in the hypothalamus that appears to be different in males and females.

Hormones: testosterone and oestrogen

Hormones are chemicals that are secreted by glands.

Testosterone is a male hormone (androgen). It determines the development of male sex organs and has been found to have behavioural effects.

- The condition congenital adrenal hyperplasia (CAH) causes high levels of male hormones in both males and females. In females, CAH has been said to result in increased aggression, preference for male toys and an increased spatial ability. However, not all studies of CAH girls show these effects.
- Animal research using rats tends to show that increasing testosterone levels causes increases in aggression.
- Body builders taking androgen steroids have been found to show higher than normal aggression scores using aggression questionnaires. However, this may have been due to other factors such as occupation. Experimental research has shown no significant differences in anger and aggression between participants taking testosterone substances and controls (Tricker et al. 1996).
- Prison research has shown links between high testosterone levels and aggressive behaviour (Dabbs et al. 1995).

Oestrogen is a female hormone that determines female sexual characteristics and menstruation. It may also have psychological and behavioural effects.

Pre-menstrual syndrome (PMS), or pre-menstrual tension (PMT), can lead to moodiness, depression, aggression and irritable behaviour. PMT has been blamed for antisocial behaviour, such as shoplifting, and even for extreme violent acts such as murder. Research has not found any consistent evidence that oestrogen is responsible for the psychological symptoms that many women report (Golombok and Fivush 1994).

Evaluation

- Some evidence suggests that biological factors affect gender-related behaviour.
- Most studies do not allow us to infer cause and effect. Maybe differences in brain structure and hormones are a result of being male or female rather than a cause of male or female behaviour.
- Biological explanations cannot explain individual differences in gender-related behaviour.
- Environmental influences should also be considered.
- Contrast the biological view with that of social learning theorists.

Social learning theory of gender

Social learning theory would suggest that gender is learned through observation and imitation. Key social learning theory concepts are described below.

Imitation

Imitation is simply copying behaviour.

Reinforcement

Positive reinforcement is when we receive something pleasant for the performance of a behaviour. Positive reinforcement acts like a reward, strengthening the learned behaviour and making it more likely to be produced again in the future. Sometimes we learn through observing the consequences for others of their behaviour. This is known as **vicarious reinforcement**. Quite a lot of evidence seems to show that boys and girls are reinforced for different behaviours.

Study

Fagot (1978) observed 24 young children at home playing with their parents. She found that parents reinforced girls for asking for help, playing close by and dressing up. Boys, on the other hand, were reinforced for playing with building bricks and were actively discouraged from doll play.

Study

Smith and Lloyd (1978) showed that mothers would treat an infant differently according to the gender they believed it to be. If told it was a boy, they would give it a hammer to play with and engage in rough activity like bouncing. If told it was a girl, they would give it a doll and behave in a more calm and soothing manner.

Identification

Identification involves the child wanting to be like a specific person and results in close observation and imitation of that person's behaviour and mannerisms.

Modelling

Modelling is the process of copying a chosen person's behaviour. The usual role model for a boy is the father, and for a girl, the mother. Children may have several models whose behaviour they try to imitate.

Knowledge check 19

Identify a behaviour associated with testosterone and a behaviour associated with oestrogen.

Examiner tip

Be able to give an everyday example of how gender-related behaviour might be vicariously reinforced.

Knowledge check 20

What is a key difference between imitation and identification?

Social learning theorists noted that observation of someone's behaviour is not on its own sufficient to lead to imitation. They understood that **cognitive factors** affect whether or not modelling takes place. Cognitive factors are thinking processes such as attention, memory and decision-making. In order to imitate someone's behaviour a child must first pay attention to it, then memorise it, then decide to imitate. The decision has been found to be affected by similarity and appropriateness.

- **Similarity** — children have been found to be more likely to imitate same-sex models. Perry and Bussey (1979) showed how female children are more likely to copy female adults, and male children are more likely to copy male adults.
- **Appropriateness** — Masters et al. (1979) showed how boys and girls were likely to copy toy choices shown by their own sex only if they were also told that the toy was appropriate for their sex. If they were told that the toy was appropriate for the other sex, then they would not choose it, despite what they had seen.

Evaluation

- Studies show that boys and girls are treated and reinforced differently.
- Cross-cultural studies (e.g. Mead) indicate that gender is socially constructed.
- The theory recognises that cognitive factors affect learning.
- Many studies of modelling have low ecological validity; they involve the use of adult strangers as models or use videos; the models are carrying out artificial behaviours in an artificial context.
- The theory does not explain why gender develops gradually over years.
- There is no explanation for why two boys or two girls who have been brought up by the same parents show different gender identities. For example, one boy may be rough and tough whilst his brother is more gentle and caring.
- The theory assumes that biology has little effect on gender development.

Cognitive approach to gender

The cognitive approach is concerned with how the child understands gender rather than the source of gender identity.

Kohlberg's cognitive developmental theory

Kohlberg suggested that a child's understanding of gender develops in a series of increasingly sophisticated stages.

- **Gender identity** At the age of 2–3 years, a child can label his/her own sex and label other people as male or female.
- **Gender stability** At the age of 3–4 years, a child realises that sex stays the same over time. However, children in this stage do not understand that gender stays the same across situations. For example, a child might think that a girl has changed into a boy because she is playing with a car. Children in this stage are also easily fooled by external appearance, for example, believing that a man who has long hair is really a woman.
- **Gender constancy (consistency)** Between the ages of 4 and 7 years, children acquire a full understanding of gender, knowing that gender stays the same across time, in different situations and despite changes in outward appearance.

Examiner tip
When answering a question on social learning theory, it is important to refer to the role of cognitive (thinking) processes.

Examiner tip
If using the Bandura Bobo doll study to answer a social learning theory question on gender, emphasise the gender aspect of the study, i.e. how Bandura found that boys were more likely to copy the behaviour if the model they observed was male.

Examiner tip
Questions about children's **understanding** of gender are asking about the cognitive approach. If a question asks for a study in which the understanding of gender was investigated, use a cognitive study.

Examiner tip
Be clear about Kohlberg's stages and what children can and cannot do at each stage.

Study

Slaby and Frey (1975) interviewed young children using a series of questions. For example, asking whether a doll or person in a photograph was male or female. This question assessed understanding of gender identity. To test gender stability, the children were asked what sex they would be when they grew up. To test gender constancy, children were asked whether or not they would be a girl or a boy if they wore opposite-sex clothes or played with opposite-sex toys. Answers to these questions confirmed the stages described by Kohlberg.

Knowledge check 21

What are three questions that you could ask children to assess their understanding of gender?

Research using other methods has confirmed that thoughts about gender may change with age. For example, Damon (1977) asked children questions about a boy called George who wanted to play with dolls and wear a dress to school. At different ages children's responses to this scenario were quite different. Four-year-olds thought it was alright for George to play with dolls; 6-year-olds had very fixed views that it was unacceptable; older children thought it was unusual, but not necessarily wrong.

Evaluation

- There is cross-cultural support for Kohlberg's three stages.
- Kohlberg's theory describes the sequence of gender development but does not explain the cause of gender development.

Gender schema theory

A **gender schema** is a unit of knowledge consisting of information such as appropriate behaviours, characteristics, occupations and roles for males and females (Martin and Halverson 1981). Initially, a child identifies what activities and toys are appropriate for his or her sex. A child then actively seeks out further own-gender information leading to the development of more complex gender schemas. Martin and Halverson (1981) propose three stages in the development of gender schemas:

- Learning what attitudes and behaviours are usually associated with each sex.
- Making links between different aspects of the schema for one's own sex. For example, knowing that if someone plays with cars, that person is also likely to wear trousers and have short hair.
- Making these links for gender schemas for both sexes.

Knowledge check 22

What is a gender schema?

Studies show that young children are more aware of own-sex activities than opposite-sex activities. For example, Boston and Levy (1991) found that young children were able to outline typically male or female activities more accurately for their own-gender activity than for the opposite-gender activity. It has also been found that children reject or misremember information that conflicts with their gender schema. Cordua et al. (1979) showed that young children remembered sex-stereotypical video content quite accurately, but misremembered the content of videos with non-sex-stereotyped content. For example, they might misremember that a doctor character was a man, even though in the video the doctor character was female.

Evaluation

- According to gender schema theory, children identify with their own sex sooner than Kohlberg suggested.
- The theory explains why children do not automatically copy a same-sex model, but first look to see whether the behaviour is appropriate.
- Boys have been found to show more extreme gender-typed behaviour than girls, which gender schema theory cannot explain.
- Cognitive theories state that gender understanding begins around 2 years of age, which does not explain why children choose to play with those of the same sex before this age.
- Cognitive theories take little account of the role of social interaction in the development of gender, assuming that the process is largely passive.

Examiner tip
You might be asked separately about Kohlberg's theory of gender or Martin and Halverson's gender schema theory. If asked a more general question about cognitive theories of gender, refer to both Kohlberg, and Martin and Halverson.

Psychodynamic approach to gender

Freud's psychoanalytic theory of gender

Freud's theory of development proposed that development takes place in psychosexual stages; at each stage the child experiences an unconscious conflict. Gender development takes place during the **phallic stage** at about 5 years. In this stage, the child's libido or psychic energy is directed towards the genital area and gender identity develops through the resolution of either the Oedipus complex (boys) or the Electra complex (girls).

Examiner tip
When answering questions about Freud's theory of gender development, focus on the phallic stage. Freud's other stages are not relevant to the development of gender.

Oedipus complex

The boy develops a desire for his mother; at the same time he is afraid of his father who he sees as a powerful rival for the mother's affection. Fearing the father's revenge, the boy becomes anxious that his father will castrate him. To resolve this conflicting desire between love for his mother and fear of castration, the boy gives up the love for his mother and identifies with his father. Freud refers to this as **identification with the aggressor**. Through this identification the boy adopts the father's male identity and assumes male characteristics. According to Freud's theory, a boy who has not resolved his Oedipus complex will be confused about his sexual identity.

Electra complex

The girl realises that she lacks a penis and thinks that she has already been castrated. The girl blames the mother. She develops **penis envy**, which leads to desire for the father who possesses what she wants. Unable to have a penis of her own, her 'penis envy' is converted into a desire for a baby (the 'penis-baby' project). In this way, the girl identifies with the mother and assumes the female role and female characteristics.

Freud saw female identification as being weaker than male identification because girls believe they have already suffered castration, so are therefore much less fearful than boys. This would suggest therefore that boys actively identify with the father, whereas for girls, the process is more passive. This active–passive difference can be seen in the gender roles as they develop, with boys becoming active, dominant and aggressive, and girls becoming quiet, passive and submissive.

Knowledge check 23
How is Freud's idea of 'identification' different from the social learning theory idea of 'identification'?

Study

The case of **Little Hans** is often used to illustrate the Oedipus complex. At the age of 4 years, Hans developed a phobia of being bitten by a horse. Hans's father, who was a friend of Freud, wrote to Freud about his child's phobia asking for his opinion. Hans particularly feared white horses with black blinkers and black mouths. Freud suggested that Hans had an unconscious fear of his father, and that the horse was merely a symbol of the father, who had a beard and wore glasses. Hans's fear of being bitten symbolised his fear of being castrated by his father. According to Freud's analysis, Hans was a little Oedipus.

Evaluation

- Hans's phobia may be better explained through classical conditioning; his fear had developed as a result of him seeing a frightening accident involving a horse.
- Freud's theory assumes that children who grow up in a household without both mother and father would have sex-role identification problems, but studies have found that children living in such 'atypical' households show traditional gender roles.
- Gender identity does not develop suddenly at the age of 4 or 5 years as Freud's theory would predict. In fact, most children show gender awareness well before that age.
- There is little or no empirical evidence to support psychodynamic theory.
- The notion of childhood sexuality is controversial.

Examiner tip

When discussing the psychodynamic explanation of gender your evaluation should focus on how well the theory explains gender and not on more general criticisms of the psychodynamic approach.

Neo-Freudian Someone who generally agrees with Freud's ideas but has reinterpreted or developed some aspect of his original theory.

Neo-Freudians (new Freudians) have developed Freud's ideas in their own views about gender. **Karen Horney** proposes that penis envy is really a desire for the power and control that males possess in society. **Erik Erikson** suggests that females do not experience penis envy and that men are actually envious of women's ability to create. **Nancy Chodorow** suggests that gender identity is based on the early mother–child relationship. Mothers identify more strongly with daughters than sons, encouraging greater closeness with daughters. As a result, female children identify via the mother with the female role and male children are encouraged to be separate and reject femininity.

Summary

- Sex is our biological status as male or female. Gender is the psychosocial role associated with being either male or female. Sex is fixed. Gender can change.

- Androgyny means a balance of masculine and feminine traits. Androgyny was measured by Bem (1974) using the BSRI.

- Sex-role stereotypes are beliefs about behaviours, attitudes and traits associated with being male and female. Seavey et al. (1975) showed how we stereotype babies according to whether we think they are male or female.

- Mead (1935) found cultural variations in gender in the Arapesh, Mundugumor and Tchambuli societies. Gender variation between cultures suggests gender is due to nurture not nature.

- The nature–nurture debate focuses on the relative importance of biology (nature) and environment (nurture) in determining gender.

- The biological explanation of gender focuses on chromosomes (male XX, female XY) and hormones (male hormones or androgens such as testosterone, and female hormones such as oestrogen). Testosterone has been linked with aggression (Dabbs et al. 1995). Oestrogen has been linked with emotional behaviour. Biopsychologists study atypical sex chromosome patterns (XXY — Klinefelter's syndrome and XO — Turner's syndrome). Comparing people with typical and atypical sex chromosome patterns might tell us whether gender is biologically determined.

- Social learning theorists say gender is learnt through reinforcement, modelling, imitation and identification. Fagot (1978) showed how boys and girls are reinforced differently by parents. Social learning theory emphasises how cognitive factors (thinking processes) affect whether or not gender-related behaviour is imitated.

- Kohlberg's three cognitive stages of gender understanding (identity, stability, constancy) were studied by Slaby and Frey (1975) using the gender concept interview. Martin and Halverson's gender

schema theory (1981) proposes that children develop increasingly sophisticated schema about gender with age, paying more attention to their own gender and rejecting gender-inconsistent information.

- Psychodynamic theorists propose that gender develops through unconscious identification with the same-sex parent. For Freud, this occurs in the phallic stage when the boy resolves the Oedipus complex and the girl resolves the Electra complex. Freud's theory is supported with the case of Little Hans.

Research methods

Planning research

Specification content

Qualitative and quantitative research and data collection techniques. Formulating research questions: stating aims; formulating hypotheses (experimental/alternative/ research). Populations and sampling: sampling techniques, including opportunity, random, stratified and systematic.

Qualitative and quantitative research

Qualitative research focuses on thoughts and feelings and usually involves some form of interview or an observation. Qualitative data are meaningful non-numerical information because they are usually collected first-hand and the information can be put into context. **Quantitative research** focuses on numerical data. Data collected in quantitative research are less meaningful because the information is narrowly focused (e.g. score in a memory test) and is taken out of context. Qualitative data can be converted into quantitative data, e.g. by categorising responses in an interview and then calculating frequencies of certain types of response.

Formulating research questions

Most research stems from other studies or arises because a researcher wants to investigate the validity of a theory. Research questions can also arise when there is a problem to be solved, e.g. where a researcher wants to test the effectiveness of a new treatment.

Stating aims

The aim of an investigation states what it is the researcher is trying to find out. The aim need not be testable but should give a clear idea of what is involved.

Examiner tip

Whenever you read about a study, consider whether the data is qualitative or quantitative. It is appropriate to discuss the relevant strengths and limitations when evaluating the study.

Knowledge check 24

What is the difference between the aim of a study and the hypothesis?

Examiner tip

In the exam, you must make sure that the hypothesis refers to exactly what is being measured (e.g. *number* of words, *time* taken to solve a problem). For an experimental study, you must include the two conditions by name (not Condition A and Condition B).

Sample The group of people being studied.

Population The larger group from which the sample is drawn.

Formulating hypotheses

The next job is for the researcher to formulate a precise testable statement — the hypothesis. A hypothesis predicts the relationship between two variables. A good hypothesis should specify clearly what the conditions of the experiment are and what exactly is to be measured.

The **research** or **alternative hypothesis** predicts that an effect will occur. This is sometimes referred to as an **experimental hypothesis** if the research method used is an experiment. After analysing the data the researcher either accepts or rejects the research hypothesis. Defining variables clearly in the hypothesis is known as **operationalisation**.

- *Incorrect hypothesis*: 'People's memory will be better if information is organised.'
- *Correct hypothesis*: 'People will recall more words from a list when the words are presented in categorised groups than when they are presented randomly.'

Populations and sampling

The term sample refers to the people (participants) who take part in research. The larger group of people from whom the sample is chosen is the **target** population. It is important that the sample represents the population so that the results can be generalised to a wider group of people than just those that have been studied. **Sampling bias** can occur where the sample is dominated by a particular sub-group in the target population, for example, mostly males.

Sampling techniques

Opportunity sample: people who are easily available.

Strength
- This method is quick and easy.

Limitation
- **Researcher bias** may occur where the researcher chooses whoever he or she wants to take part. The participants may be a group of similar people, even the researcher's friends; the sample is unlikely to be representative, making it difficult to generalise.

Examiner tip

Students often confuse random and opportunity sampling. Using whoever is available is opportunity. A random sample has to involve some kind of 'lottery' to decide who should be in the sample.

Random sample: every member of the target population has an equal chance of being chosen. This can be done by drawing names from a hat or by giving everyone a number and using a computer programme to generate random numbers.

Strength
- No researcher bias as the researcher does not control who is chosen.

Limitation
- The sample may still not be representative; by chance there might be more males in the sample than females.

Stratified sample: the researcher randomly selects participants from different sub-groups (strata) within the population. Each sub-group is represented proportionately. For example, if the target population includes 100 males and 200 females then the sample should have one male for every two females.

Strength
- It is likely to give a representative sample.

Limitation
- It is sometimes difficult to identify the sub-groups. It is also time-consuming.

Systematic sample: every *n*th member of the target population is selected, for example, every third employee on a payroll.

Strength
- No researcher bias.

Limitation
- The sample may not necessarily be representative.

Examiner tip

A question may ask you to define a sampling technique, 'Outline what is meant by x sampling', or ask you how a particular type of sample might be obtained in a given situation, e.g. using nurses in a hospital. Check the question carefully before you start to answer — is it asking for a simple definition, or about a specific situation?

Knowledge check 25

Which sampling technique involves random selection from different sub-groups within a population?

Experimental methods

Specification content

Field, laboratory and quasi-experiments; ecological validity. Independent and dependent variables. Extraneous and confounding variables. Experimental designs: repeated, matched and independent. Controls including counterbalancing and random allocation.

Field, laboratory and quasi-experiments

In an experiment one variable is changed or manipulated and the effect on another variable is measured. The variable that the researcher manipulates is the independent variable **(IV)**, and the variable the researcher measures is the dependent variable **(DV)**. All other variables should be controlled. This control allows the researcher to make assumptions about a cause-and-effect relationship between the IV and the DV.

Independent variable The variable the researcher manipulates.
Dependent variable The variable the researcher measures.

Field experiment

A field experiment takes place in a natural environment. Field experiments are high in **ecological validity** because they involve the study of behaviour in a real-life situation. A good example is Bickman's research (1974), where people were asked to pick up litter by someone dressed either in ordinary clothes or in a uniform.

Laboratory experiment

Laboratory experiments take place in a constant environment with external variables such as noise and distractions controlled; so each participant performs in exactly the same conditions. Laboratory experiments can result in artificial behaviour because people behave differently when they know they are being studied. In addition, experimental tasks are often highly artificial. As a result, laboratory experiments may lack **ecological validity**.

Knowledge check 26

In which type of experiment is there the greatest amount of control so that the cause and effect relationship between the two variables can be clearly demonstrated?

Examiner tip

When you have to identify the IV and DV in a study, first decide what the researcher is measuring — this is the DV. The other variable that changes must therefore be the IV.

Quasi-experiment

In quasi-experiments there is no random allocation to conditions and no directly controlled manipulation of the IV. This would occur when an experimenter compares the performance of two different groups of people, for example, males and females. In quasi-experiments the researcher cannot draw such clear conclusions about cause and effect as in experiments in which there is direct manipulation of the IV.

Independent and dependent variables

The **independent variable (IV)** is the variable the researcher manipulates. The **dependent variable (DV)** is the variable the researcher measures. Using the example of recall for a list of words that are either organised into categories or randomly presented, the IV would be whether or not the words are categorised, and the DV would be the number of words recalled.

IV and DV examples

An experiment to see whether people will wait longer in a queue if music is playing or not

IV   whether music is playing or not
DV   waiting time in minutes

An experiment to see whether people who do crosswords more than twice a week score more highly in a spelling test than people who do not

IV   whether people do crosswords more than twice a week or not
DV   spelling test score

Extraneous variable Any variable, other than the independent variable, that might affect the dependent variable.

Examiner tip

In the examination you may have to write a set of standardised instructions, which are given to participants before they carry out the experimental task, to explain what they have to do. They should be written clearly, in everyday language, and should make it clear that the participants can withdraw from the study at any time.

Extraneous and confounding variables: control

An extraneous variable is any variable, other than the independent variable, that might affect the dependent variable. An extraneous variable needs to be controlled by the researcher so that it does not become a **confounding variable**, spoiling the results of the study. If results are confounded by an uncontrolled extraneous variable, then we cannot say that the IV has affected the DV and so cannot draw sensible conclusions.

Examples of extraneous variables that should be controlled are: time allowed for completion of a task; outside noise; presence of other people; use of different materials in each condition; different experimenters for each condition; variations in wording of instructions.

Where the experimenter knowingly or unknowingly treats different participants differently, this is known as **experimenter bias**. To control for experimenter bias it is sensible to use written **standardised instructions** so that each participant has the same experience during the experiment. Another strategy for coping with experimenter bias is to carry out **double-blind research**, where the researcher who actually carries out the experiment does not know the aim of the research.

Experimental designs

There are three experimental designs in psychological research.

Repeated or related measures design

The same people are used in both conditions and their performances are compared.

Strengths
- There are no individual differences or participant variables.
- Fewer participants are needed overall.

Limitations
- **Order effects** may occur, i.e. participants' performance in the second condition may be affected by their experience of the first condition. They may improve their performance in the second condition because they have had a practice (**practice effect**); or they may be worse in the second condition because they are tired or bored (**fatigue effect**). To control for order effects the researcher should **counterbalance** the conditions, with half the participants doing Condition A then B, and the other half doing Condition B and then A.
- Participants may guess what the study is about and may behave differently than if they had not known.
- Different sets of materials may be required.

Independent groups design

Different participants perform in each condition and their performances are compared. Here it is important to randomly allocate participants to the conditions to avoid researcher bias. **Random allocation** means that everyone has an equal chance of being in either condition. It can be done by drawing names out of a hat.

Strengths
- No order effects.
- Participants cannot guess the purpose of the study.
- Only one set of stimulus materials is required.

Limitations
- Individual differences or participant variables may affect the results. To control for this use **random allocation**.
- More participants are needed overall.

Matched pairs design

Different people perform in each condition, but they are matched in ways that matter for the experiment, for example, sex, age and IQ. For each participant in Condition A, there must be a matching participant in the other condition.

Strengths
- Individual differences or participant variables are reduced.
- There are no order effects.
- Participants cannot guess the purpose of the study.
- Only one set of materials is needed.

Knowledge check 27

How should researchers control for order effects in a repeated measures design experiment?

Knowledge check 28

How should researchers control for individual differences in an independent groups design?

Replication Carrying out a study again in exactly the same way to see whether the findings are the same — a very important part of the scientific process.

Subjective Based on personal opinion; the opposite is *objective*: based on observable fact.

Limitations
- It is difficult and time-consuming to match pairs.
- No two people are exactly the same. Therefore matching cannot eliminate individual differences altogether.

Strengths of the experimental method
- A **cause-and-effect relationship** between the IV and DV can be determined.
- Strictly controlled procedures mean that replication is possible to check whether the findings are **reliable**.
- It is more ethical than methods where participants are unaware that they are being studied.
- Measures are **objective**, that is, can be directly observed.

Limitations of the experimental method
- Experiments often lack ecological validity because they test behaviour in a way in which it might not occur in real life.
- Participants may pick up clues as to the purpose of the experiment and respond to these **demand characteristics** by behaving differently to how they would normally behave. Some participants try to 'make the experiment work'; others might try to 'mess the experiment up'.

Non-experimental methods

Specification content

Self-report methods: questionnaire construction; types of interviews. Correlation studies; the difference between experiments and correlations. Observational studies. Content analysis. Case studies. Pilot studies.

Self-report methods

This is where participants report on their own behaviour, feelings or opinions. Self-report methods are often described as subjective because they are based on the participant's opinion. Questionnaires and interviews are both examples of self-report methods.

Questionnaires

Questionnaires are used to study behaviours and attitudes that cannot be directly observed. Questionnaire items should be clear and unambiguous.

Closed questions: there are a fixed number of optional answers.

Example: Do you think that cannabis should be legalised?

     YES   NO   DON'T KNOW

Closed questions give data that are easy to analyse. Answers, however, may have low validity because people cannot give their own answer, and instead have to go for the nearest option.

Open questions: respondents can put any answer they like.

Example: How much alcohol do you drink per week on average?

Open questions give more meaningful and valid information as people can put the answer they want, but the data are difficult to analyse.

Strengths of the questionnaire method
- Data can be collected quickly.
- The method can be replicated.
- There are no ethical problems as participants know they are taking part.

Limitations of the questionnaire method
- It is difficult to construct a good questionnaire.
- Social desirability — respondents try to make themselves appear to be 'nice'.
- 'Yea' saying — a bias towards agreement on questionnaires.
- Response set — people just choose all 'yes' or all 'no' answers.

Interviews

Structured interview: pre-prepared questions are asked in a fixed order. If each participant answers the same questions, the data can be analysed easily and the interview stays focused. However, in a structured interview there is no chance to ask any extra questions if an interesting issue arises during the interview.

Unstructured interview: there is an aim but no fixed questions; the researcher can ask any questions that are appropriate. Unstructured interviews produce more detailed and valid data, but responses are all different and therefore difficult to analyse and the interview may go off track.

Strengths of the interview method
- It is useful for the study of opinions and past experiences.
- It produces many data.

Limitations of the interview method
- It is a self-report method and therefore subjective.
- It tells us little about the causes of behaviour.
- The interviewer's personality and style are likely to affect the outcome.

Correlation studies

Correlation is a statistical technique used to measure the relationship between two variables. Correlations are usually represented in the form of a scattergram.

In a **positive correlation** (see Figure 4), as one variable increases the other variable increases. In a **negative correlation,** as one variable increases, the other variable decreases.

Correlations allow us to make predictions: for example, if we know there is a positive correlation between number of days' holiday and happiness, then we could predict that someone who has lots of holidays will be happier and vice versa.

Examiner tip

In the examination, if you are asked to write a *closed* question, make sure you give the optional responses along with the question. If asked for an *open* question, make sure it cannot be answered with a simple 'Yes' or 'No'.

Knowledge check 29

Which type of interview is likely to gain the more interesting and meaningful information about a specific individual?

Strengths of the correlation method
- Correlations show a relationship in circumstances where it would not be possible to do an experimental manipulation.
- Correlations enable predictions about behaviour.

Limitations of the correlation method
- Correlations do not tell us that one variable causes another — they do not show cause and effect.

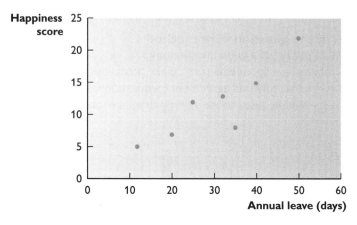

Figure 4 Scattergram to show the relationship between the number of days of annual holiday and happiness score

Key differences between an experiment and a correlation study

Experiment: control of extraneous variables; shows cause and effect.

Correlation: no control of extraneous variables; does not show cause and effect.

Observational studies

In a **natural observation**, observations take place in a natural environment, for example in a playground or at a football match. Extraneous variables are not controlled, but there is high validity because the behaviour is real behaviour in a real setting. **Controlled observations** are conducted under controlled conditions with extraneous variables eliminated. This control allows for replication, but it means the data may have less validity because the situation is artificial.

In a **participant observation** the observer joins in the action with those being observed, allowing behaviour to be understood in context. Participant observation can result in loss of objectivity because the observer is too involved in what is going on. The observer's presence may also affect the outcome. In **non-participant observation**, the observer merely watches and does not take part, allowing the observer to be more objective.

In an **overt observation** people know that they are being observed. This is ethical but may lead to artificial behaviour if people know that they are being watched. This

Examiner tip
Correlations are useful where it would not be possible to do an experiment. For example, it is possible to correlate stress levels with days off work sick, but you could not deliberately cause stress to one group of participants to see if they have more time off work sick than a control group.

is known as an **observer effect**. Covert **observation** is where people do not know they are being observed. This avoids an **observer effect**, but could be unethical because people have not given their consent.

Observational recording techniques

Observational researchers often use a category system, breaking down the target behaviour into operational categories. For example, if the target behaviour is 'aggression', the **behavioural categories** might be hitting, smacking, kicking, hair-pulling. To be useful, category systems should be clear and unambiguous. Any instances of these behaviours can be recorded on a tally chart.

Observers may make **continuous recordings,** noting down every instance of the target behaviour as it occurs. Continuous recording is appropriate where the target behaviour occurs as a separate event (e.g. a hit or a smack), but is not suitable for recording behaviours that are on-going (e.g. playing with another child). For such behaviours, **time sampling** is a useful technique. Here the total observation time is divided into time intervals (e.g. every minute), and at each time interval the behaviour is noted.

Observer bias is where the researcher's beliefs or expectations lead them to be biased in their observations. For example, if a researcher expects boys to be more aggressive than girls, this could affect the way an action is interpreted during the observation.

To avoid this bias two researchers often observe side by side but record separately. Ideally, both sets of observations should be the same. This is known as **inter-observer reliability**.

Strengths of the observational method
- Data have high ecological validity.
- It is useful for studying social behaviours.

Limitations of the observational method
- There may be observer bias.
- There may be an observer effect.
- It does not show cause and effect (unless part of an experiment).
- It is time-consuming.
- Ethical problems — lack of consent, lack of right to withdraw, invasion of privacy.

Content analysis

Content analysis involves systematic measurement of aspects of media communications, such as books and television programmes. Various units can be analysed, e.g. number of male/female characters, words, ideas. The data are usually recorded in the form of frequencies.

Strengths of the content analysis method
- It is appropriate for any form of media.
- There are not usually any ethical problems.

Covert Hidden from view.

Knowledge check 30

What is meant by objectivity in relation to the observational method?

Examiner tip

If asked about designing an observation, refer to the category system you would use. Practise doing this now. What behavioural categories would you use if you were investigating 'friendly behaviours in a primary school playground'?

Examiner tip

Be able to explain exactly how inter-observer reliability would be established.

Knowledge check 31

Why are there not usually any ethical problems involved in content analysis?

Limitations of the content analysis method

- Behaviour is being studied out of context. For example, studying the content of a politician's speech does not take account of the mood of the audience.
- Categories are decided in advance and are based on the researcher's expectations.
- Interpretation may be subjective.

Case studies

Case studies are usually conducted by clinical psychologists and involve in-depth research with a single person or a small group. Several forms of data can be used including observations, interviews, psychological testing etc. Medical and school history records might also be useful depending on the situation. The psychologist produces a description of the case, followed by an interpretation of the findings. In clinical cases there might also be some recommendation for future treatment.

Examiner tip

Avoid evaluating the case study method by saying simply that 'the results cannot be generalised'. Make sure you get the best possible mark by offering explanation. In this case you could add '...as the data is gathered from one individual who may not be at all typical and therefore the results would not apply to other people'.

Strengths of the case study method
- The data are rich in detail.
- It enables a long-term view.
- It has high validity because the research is based on a real person and his or her real experiences.
- A single case can be used to challenge theory.

Limitations of the case study method
- Results cannot be generalised.
- Often based on recall, which may not be reliable.
- The researcher's expectations may affect their interpretation — **researcher bias**.
- Ethical issues such as consent, right to withdraw, protection from harm and confidentiality need to be carefully considered.

Pilot studies

Pilot study A small-scale investigation carried out **before** the main investigation.

A pilot study is a small-scale investigation carried out as a preliminary to the main investigation. The pilot study allows the researcher to determine whether there are any problems with the design or materials so that adjustments can be made before carrying out the full-scale investigation. Pilot studies can be used for any type of investigation: an experimental procedure can be trialled with a couple of participants to see that they understand the standardised instructions; a questionnaire can be trialled with a few respondents to see whether they understand the wording of the questions; a researcher may carry out a pilot observation to see whether or not categories are appropriate.

Representing data and descriptive statistics

Specification content

Use of measures of central tendency (mean, median and mode) and measures of dispersion (range and standard deviation). Calculation of mean, median, mode and

AQA(B) AS Psychology

range. Correlation as a description of the relationship between two variables. Positive, negative and zero correlations. Appropriate use of tabular and graphical displays: tables, bar charts, graphs, scattergrams.

Descriptive statistics

In an examination you may be asked to perform simple calculations so you need to know how to calculate the mean, median, mode and range. You will not be asked to calculate the standard deviation in an examination, but you need to know what the SD means and how it differs from the range.

Measures of central tendency

A measure of central tendency is a single figure that is used to show an average score for a set of scores.

Central tendency Typical or average score.

There are three measures of central tendency:
● the mean
● the median
● the mode

To calculate **the mean** ($\bar{x}$) add up all the scores and divide by the number of scores. The mean is very sensitive because it uses all the scores, but it can be distorted by an extreme or **anomalous** score.

The median is the middle score when all the scores have been put into order from lowest to highest. If there is no middle score, add together the two middle scores and divide by two. The median is not distorted by extreme scores, but is not as sensitive as the mean because not all scores are used in the calculation.

The mode is simply the most frequent score in a set of scores. It is easy to find but is a very insensitive measure and not very useful: for example, there may be more than one mode or there may not be one at all.

Knowledge check 32

Calculate the mean, median and mode for the following set of scores: 6, 3, 2, 2, 3, 4, 4, 5, 2, 14.

Measures of dispersion

As well as finding an average score, it is important to know how much spread there is in a set of scores. Two measures of dispersion or spread are:
● the range
● the standard deviation

Dispersion Spread of scores.

Knowledge check 33

What is the range for the set of scores given in Knowledge check 32?

To find the **range,** subtract the lowest score from the highest score. The range can be distorted by an extremely high or low score, leading us to believe that a set of scores is spread out — even when the majority of the scores are close to the mean.

The **standard deviation (SD)** takes account of every score in a set of scores, thus representing the spread for the scores as a whole. A low SD means that the scores are not spread out, whereas a high SD means the scores are widely spread. The calculation for the SD takes into account the distance of each score from the mean and is much more sensitive than the range.

Knowledge check 34

Why do researchers tend to use the standard deviation as a measure of dispersion rather than the range?

Examiner tip

Remember that, in the examination, marks are awarded for axis labels and titles as well as for plotting the graphs.

Representing data

You will need to be familiar with the different methods of representing data and should be prepared to sketch simple graphs and tables in the examination.

Tabular displays: summary tables

Tables should have a clear title and column headings. The title must refer to the two conditions by name and include the unit of measurement (i.e. what the numbers refer to).

	Males	Females
Average weekly ice-cream consumption (in millilitres) for males and females	60	180

Average weekly ice-cream consumption (ml)

Also be prepared to write a short verbal summary: 'Notice from the above table that females, on average, consume more ice-cream in a week than males'.

Examiner tip

If you are asked to draw a graph to display data from an experiment with two conditions, you should draw a bar chart using either the mean scores (or median/mode) or the total scores for each condition.

Graphical displays

- bar charts
- line graphs
- scattergrams

Bar charts are used to show frequencies in columns with the frequency on the vertical axis and the variable on the horizontal axis. The bar chart shown in Figure 5 illustrates the information about ice-cream consumption shown in the table.

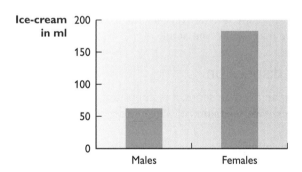

Figure 5 Average weekly ice-cream consumption (in millilitres) for males and females

Line graphs show a relationship between independent and dependent variables, with the IV on the horizontal axis and the DV on the vertical axis. A line graph is only appropriate where the variable is continuous. Contrast this with the bar graph of means; it would not be meaningful to join the means for males and females as they are quite separate. The line graph in Figure 6 shows the average ice-cream consumption (ml) for males in the months March to November.

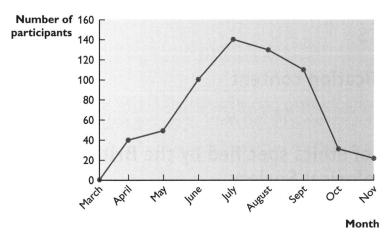

Figure 6 Average ice-cream consumption (ml) for males from March to November

Scattergrams are used for correlational data. One variable is plotted on each axis with each pair shown as a single point on the scattergram. The pattern of points indicates a positive, negative or zero correlation, as shown in Figure 7.

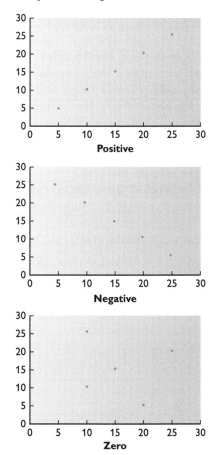

> **Examiner tip**
> Remember, scattergrams are used only when you are displaying data from a correlation. Each point on your scattergram represents a pair of scores, usually a person, with one of their scores on the x-axis and their other score on the y-axis.

Figure 7 Scattergrams to show positive, negative and zero correlations

Ethics

Specification content

An awareness of the code of ethics in psychology as specified by the British Psychological Society. The application of the code of ethics in psychological research.

Code of ethics specified by the British Psychological Society

The Code of Ethics and Conduct (2006), set out by the British Psychological Society (BPS), protects participants, patients and clients, maintains professional standards, provides a framework and guides decisions about appropriate conduct. The guidelines cover the professional and research activities of all psychologists. They apply to everyone carrying out psychological research, including students. You need to be aware of ethical issues relating to psychological research and follow the guidelines in any practical activities.

Knowledge check 35

Give three reasons why psychologists need a code of ethics.

Applying the code of ethics in research

The code specifies four headings: respect, competence, responsibility, integrity.

- **Respect** — psychologists should respect individuals and avoid unfairness and prejudice. Information about people should be kept **confidential**. **Informed consent** must be sought, meaning that participants should know what they are consenting to. Parental consent is normally obtained for participants under 16 years old. **Privacy** should be respected in observations. **Deception** should be avoided wherever possible. If participants must be deceived, then they should be informed as soon as possible. Participants should have a **right to withdraw** either themselves or their data from research at any time.
- **Competence** — only qualified psychologists should give advice.
- **Responsibility** — participants must be **protected from harm**. Psychologists must **debrief** research participants after the investigation, telling them details of the research and its purpose.
- **Integrity** — psychologists should be honest and maintain professional boundaries.

Examiner tip

If asked about ethical issues in relation to a study described in the question, you must apply your answer to the study given in order to get full marks. It is not enough to give a general definition or explanation of the issue.

An easy way to remember the key ethical issues in psychological research is to use the memory technique **CCDDPPW**:
- Consent
- Confidentiality
- Deception
- Debrief
- Protection
- Privacy
- Withdrawal

- Qualitative research produces non-numerical, meaningful data whereas quantitative research produces numerical data that is easy to analyse.

- The research aim is general whereas the hypothesis is operationalised as a precise, testable statement.

- A sample should reflect the target population; sampling can be opportunity, random, stratified or systematic.

- Types of experiments are field, laboratory and quasi. Every experiment has an independent variable (IV — manipulated by researcher) and a dependent variable (DV — measured by researcher). There are three experimental designs: repeated measures; independent groups; matched pairs. Counterbalancing and random allocation are techniques of experimental control. Results of an experiment can be confounded if extraneous variables are not controlled. Experiments show cause and effect.

- Self-report methods involve participants giving information about themselves using questionnaires or interviews. Questionnaires can have open questions (any answer) or closed questions (options to choose). Interviews can be structured (fixed questions) or unstructured (with an aim but no fixed questions).

- Correlation involves testing the mathematical relationship between two variables — unlike an experiment there is no manipulation of variables so no cause and effect can be established.

- Observational research can be natural or controlled, overt or covert, participant or non-participant. Observers use category systems to tally behaviour. Two observers work side by side to check for inter-observer reliability.

- Content analysis involves the systematic observation and measurement of media content.

- Case studies are in-depth investigations of a single person/small group and are usually done in clinical contexts.

- A pilot study is a small-scale study done before the main study to test the method, materials, and so on.

- Descriptive statistics include measures of central tendency — mean, median, mode, and measures of dispersion — range and standard deviation.

- Data can be displayed in tables, bar charts, line graphs and scattergrams.

- The BPS code of ethics protects participants, maintains standards and provides guidelines for psychologists.

- Ethical issues are respect, competence, responsibility and integrity. Practical issues in research include: consent, confidentiality, deception, debriefing, protection, privacy and right to withdraw (CCDDPPW).

Questions & Answers

In this section of the guide there are six questions — two on Approaches, two on Gender Development and two on Research Methods. Each question is worth 20 marks. You should allow 30 minutes when answering each question. This section is structured as follows:

- sample question in the style in which they appear on the Unit 1 question paper
- analysis of the question, explaining what is expected in each sub-section of the question
- examples of student responses; these have been selected to illustrate particular strengths and limitations

Examiner comments

All student responses are followed by examiner comments, preceded by the icon .

Examiner comments explain how the marks have been awarded, aspects of the answer that are especially creditworthy and possible areas for improvement.

The examination

The Unit 1 examination is 1½ hours long and you have to answer three questions: one on Approaches (including Biopsychology), one on Gender Development and one on Research Methods. Each question carries *20 marks* so you should allow 30 minutes for each question in the examination.

The Approaches and Gender Development questions are structured, which means that there are several sub-sections to each question. The first sub-sections are usually short-answer questions worth *1, 2, 3* or *4 marks*. These are followed by a final sub-section that requires extended writing for *10 marks*.

Short-answer questions

- Commands like 'Identify', 'State', 'Name', 'Suggest' and 'Give' require the briefest answers.
- Commands like 'Outline' and 'Describe' require straightforward description.
- Commands like 'Explain' and 'Distinguish' require some analysis or elaboration of concepts. In the case of 'Distinguish', you need to explain the difference(s) between two points.
- The command 'Briefly discuss' requires some description and some evaluation or criticism and is usually worth *4 or 5 marks*.
- If asked to 'Describe a study' for *4 marks*, you should refer explicitly to the aim and method, results and conclusion.
- If asked to 'Outline a study' for *2/3 marks* you should refer to the method/procedure and the results/findings.

Examples of short-answer questions

'Identify **two** assumptions of the humanistic approach.'

'Explain what is meant by *free will*.'

'Give an example of modelling.'

'State what is meant by *qualitative research*.'

'Outline what psychologists mean by the term *androgyny*.'

'Describe **one** study in which classical conditioning was investigated.'

'Briefly discuss **one** limitation of the case study method.'

'Distinguish between imitation and identification.'

Long-answer questions

These are worth *10 marks*. A typical 10-mark question would ask you to 'Describe and evaluate' a theory, an explanation or some research. In 10-mark questions, *5 marks* are for description and *5 marks* are for evaluation/analysis/application. In the evaluation, you should present strengths and limitations. If relevant, you should support what you say with reference to evidence and explain how the evidence relates to the topic. You can also get evaluation marks by comparing — for example, introducing an opposing theory to illustrate the limitations of the theory you are discussing. You should aim to spend plenty of time on this sub-section of the question in the examination.

In the 10-mark questions you will be assessed on your ability to communicate. You should therefore make sure that your answer is properly structured into sentences and paragraphs, and pay attention to your spelling. If a 10-mark question asks you to 'refer to evidence' or 'refer to an alternative explanation', there will be a limit to the number of marks that you will be awarded if you do not comply with that instruction.

Mark schemes for 10-mark questions are banded into 'very good', 'good', 'average' and 'poor' bands. This means that the examiner will not only consider each individual point that you make, but will also make a global assessment of the answer as a whole. Students who show lots of knowledge and make many evaluation points but do not present a well-argued response will generally be awarded a lower mark than they might have been given. This is because the answer as a whole is better suited to the 'average' band rather than the 'good' band.

Scenario questions

In some questions you must use your knowledge by applying what you have learned about psychology to a novel situation. For example, a question might include a scenario about someone who is on a scary roller-coaster ride. In this case, you might be required to use your knowledge of the autonomic nervous system to explain the physiological reactions of the person in the scenario. For example, you could describe how the person's heart-rate would increase and their digestion would slow down. This sort of question tests the application of knowledge.

Research Methods questions

Unit 1 has one full question on Research Methods. This is more heavily structured than the other questions, consisting of several sub-sections requiring short answers. There is no 10-mark sub-section in the Research Methods question. In addition to the full question on Research Methods, there may be sub-sections assessing knowledge and understanding of Research Methods and practical psychology in other questions. For example, there may be a Gender Development question in which you are asked how gender stereotyping has been studied by psychologists.

Assessment objectives

Examination boards use the term 'assessment objective' (AO) to refer to the different types of skills that you are expected to demonstrate in examinations. Your teacher might have told you about AO1, AO2 and AO3 skills.

- AO1 refers to knowledge and understanding.
- AO2 refers to analysis and evaluation and the application of knowledge to novel situations.
- AO3 refers to knowledge and understanding of Research Methods and practical psychology.

You should not worry too much about these different skills in the examination. In most cases the wording of the question will lead you to demonstrate the necessary skills. Only the following two types of question require you to think about AO skills:

- In 10-mark questions, *5 marks* are for description (AO1) and *5 marks* are for evaluation, analysis and application (AO2). In a 10-mark question, you should aim to present a balance of description and evaluation/analysis/application. These will usually ask you to 'Describe and evaluate' or 'Discuss'.
- 'Briefly discuss' for *3*, *4* or *5 marks* — here there would normally be *1* or *2 marks* for description (AO1) and 2 or *3 marks* for evaluation, analysis and application (AO2).

Question 1 Approaches (I)

> **(a) What do humanistic psychologists mean by the term *conditions of worth?* Give an example of how a teacher might impose conditions of worth on her pupils.** (2 marks)

This is asking you to do two things and you would get a mark for each. First you need to state what is meant by the term. Second, you need to give an example relating to the question. Questions asking for an example will usually ask you to give an example in a specific context; in this case, the example is relating to a school situation.

> **(b) Marylou and Marianne are identical twins. When they were young, people could not tell them apart. Now that they are in their 50s, it is easy to tell them apart because Marylou is very slim with fine clear skin, whereas Marianne weighs a lot more and has skin that is heavily veined and lined.**
>
> **With reference to both Marylou and Marianne, explain what is meant by the terms *genotype* and *phenotype.*** (4 marks)

There are two distinct requirements. First you need to define the terms 'genotype' and 'phenotype'. Each correct definition is worth 1 mark. For the other 2 marks you need to link your definitions to the scenario taking care to refer to both the characters for full marks.

> **(c) Describe how cognitive psychologists use models to explain internal mental processes.** (4 marks)

This tests your knowledge of how science works and practical psychology by asking you about what cognitive psychologists do when they are studying mental processes. You need to explain what a model is, give an example of one and say what it shows about internal mental processes.

> **(d) Describe and evaluate the behaviourist approach in psychology. Refer to *one* other approach in your answer.** (10 marks)

Here you are expected to show your knowledge of the behaviourist approach by offering a clear description. Remember it is always important to use any specialist terminology — this shows you have been studying the topic. Half of the marks in these straightforward extended writing questions are for knowledge and description. The remaining marks are for evaluation, i.e. presenting strengths and limitations and using evidence to support what you say. In this question you are also invited to 'refer to one other approach' in your answer. This instruction is not meant to make the question any harder, but is meant to help you by suggesting that you compare the behaviourist approach with another approach as a way of obtaining more marks for evaluation and analysis. It is important to remember that if you fail to comply with any instruction asking you to 'refer to another...', or 'refer to evidence...', then you will gain a maximum of 6 marks however good the rest of the answer may be.

Student A

(a) Humanistic psychologists say that conditions of worth are when a person does not feel loved and accepted. A teacher might do this by not accepting and valuing the pupils in her class who are naughty. a

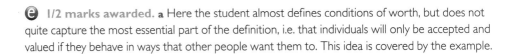

🅔 1/2 marks awarded. **a** Here the student almost defines conditions of worth, but does not quite capture the most essential part of the definition, i.e. that individuals will only be accepted and valued if they behave in ways that other people want them to. This idea is covered by the example.

> **(b)** A genotype is the person's genes that they have. **b** These are identical twins and so they have identical genes (100% the same), which means that they have identical genotypes. **c** The phenotype is the final result and these twins look different by the time they reach the age of 50 years.

🅔 2/4 marks awarded. **b** The definition of a genotype is just about sufficient to gain a mark and **c** the student correctly states that the twins have identical genotypes for a second mark. The definition of a phenotype is not explicit enough for further credit, and is not explained in the attempt to link back to the text. It does look as if the student knows what a phenotype is, but unfortunately he/she has not explained the issue of the interaction between genes and environment.

> **(c)** Cognitive psychologists use models of memory to explain internal mental processes. A model is a theory but is presented as a flowchart with arrows going from one section to another. **d** In memory, for instance, there are three stages in the model: sensory memory, short-term memory and long-term memory. **e** Once the cognitive psychologist has come up with the model, it means that other psychologists can use it to design their own studies of memory. **f**

🅔 3/4 marks awarded. The first sentence is entirely redundant because it simply repeats the question. **d** In the second sentence the student shows understanding of what a model is in this context, **e** and in the next sentence goes on to amplify this point in an example, the multi-store model of memory. **f** The final sentence gives a basic but quite sound description of how the model is used. Although not always well expressed, this is actually a good answer. Various points might have been made to secure the extra mark, e.g. that internal mental processes cannot be seen and therefore need to be made more tangible; or that models are working hypotheses based on inference.

> **(d)** The behaviourist approach includes classical and operant conditioning. Behaviourists believe that all behaviour is learnt **g** and that we should not study anything that cannot be seen; **h** for example, we should not study thinking processes and memory and so on as these are internal mental processes and so there have to be models used to explain them. Classical conditioning was devised by Pavlov who studied dog salivation and found that the dog would produce saliva to the sound of a bell because the bell was always presented at the same time as the food, **i** which naturally would produce salivation. This study has been called unethical because the dog was tied up in a harness and had a tube fixed into its throat. However, it is better to do this kind of study with animals than to do it with people. This is one of the troubles with the behaviourist approach because they use animals and this is not useful to tell us about human behaviour and learning. **j** They didn't really do any research with humans and so it is difficult to generalise. The behaviourist approach is no longer as popular as it was but it did gain a scientific reputation for psychology because of the methods being controlled and laboratory based. **k**

ⓔ **5/10 marks awarded (AO1 = 3, AO2 = 2).** The answer is not well organised; there are some inaccuracies and it sometimes goes off track. However, there is some useful description and evaluation of the approach. Notice how the student makes the fairly common mistake of using material from a previous sub-section on internal mental processes, apparently forgetting what this sub-section of the question is asking. He/she realises the mistake and soon gets back on track. Interestingly this detour into internal mental processes could have been used to good effect here by making a link between the behaviourist approach and the cognitive approach for more evaluation marks. As it is, the student has not mentioned another approach at all, and therefore could not get more than 6 marks overall.

g h i The following three points were awarded credit for description: the basic principle that all behaviour is learnt; the idea that only outward behaviour should be the subject of psychological study and why; the knowledge of the basic procedure of classical conditioning, although this is not done well. The evaluation is scattered about the answer and some of it relates more to Pavlov's research than to the behaviourist approach itself. The point about ethics is not really of relevance for this question, so does not gain credit. Evaluation credit was awarded for the following: **j** the problem of generalising from animal research and **k** the enhancement of the scientific reputation of psychology.

Total for this question: 11/20 marks — approximately grade C/D

Student B

(a) The term 'conditions of worth' refers to the idea that people will only be valued by others if they behave in acceptable ways. **a** The teacher might say to a child in her class that she will only want him in her class next year if he gets an A grade in his AS examination. **b**

ⓔ **2/2 marks awarded. a b** Here the student defines the term clearly and gives a good example.

(b) A genotype is a person's genetic make-up. **c** Identical or MZ twins are from the same fertilised egg and therefore have an identical genetic make-up, so Marylou and Marianne share 100% of their genes in common and have the same genotype. **d** A phenotype is the expression of the genotype in the individual and is the result of the interaction between the genotype and the environment. **c** Marylou and Marianne have different phenotypes, **d** which is why they look different even though they have the same genotype.

ⓔ **4/4 marks awarded. c** Both terms are defined clearly using correct terminology and **d** both are linked precisely to the cases of Marylou and Marianne.

(c) Internal mental processes like memory cannot be directly observed; therefore cognitive psychology proposes models which are really hypotheses about the structure and organisation of thinking processes. **e** One example is the multi-store model of memory proposed by Atkinson and Shiffrin in 1968. This is a theory about how memory is organised. **f** The model provides a framework for further investigation, stimulating research by other memory researchers. **g**

(d) The behaviourist approach became popular in the US where psychologists like Pavlov and Skinner carried out controlled scientific experiments about learning using animals. **h** All behaviourist research takes place in controlled conditions so that variables can be isolated and cause and effect can be determined. Behaviourists believe that all behaviour is learnt **i** and behaviour depends on consequences. **j** In a typical operant conditioning study, Skinner showed how learning bar-pressing behaviour in rats depended on whether or not the rat received a food pellet as reinforcement. Rats would rapidly learn that the action of bar-pressing resulted in a pleasant consequence, so they would repeat the action. Skinner called this positive reinforcement. **k**

Behaviourists also assume that only external behaviour is valid subject matter for psychologists if psychology is to be scientific. **l** As such they restricted their observations to outward behaviour and did not study emotions and thoughts which some people like Freud would consider of great importance. **m** In this way there is a great difference between the behaviourists and the psychodynamic psychologists like Freud, whose study of the unconscious would have been strongly criticised by behaviourists for being totally unscientific.

The behaviourists can be credited with making psychology respectable as a science **n** but have been criticised for neglecting the importance of mental life. **o** In choosing to study animal behaviour in highly controlled artificial conditions, their research could be said to have little validity in relation to everyday human behaviour. **p** The behaviourists have also been criticised for taking a mechanical view of human beings, assuming that people are responding machines that can be controlled by reinforcement, and that we have no free will. **q**

Taken as a whole, this answer provides an interesting description that covers most of the assumptions of the behaviourist approach and includes some well-argued evaluation and analysis. The slight inaccuracy of placing Pavlov in the USA is inconsequential to the content and therefore does not affect the credit awarded.

Total for this question: 20/20 marks — grade A

Question 2 **Approaches (II)**

(a) Sally often watches her mother brushing her hair and putting on her make-up. According to social learning theory, Sally might imitate her mother's actions but this would depend on mediating cognitive factors.

State what social learning theorists mean by mediating cognitive factors, and suggest two ways in which mediating factors might affect Sally's behaviour in this situation. **(3 marks)**

⒠ This is an application question where you are required to show your understanding by applying what you know, in this case about social learning theory, to a novel situation. Notice the two parts to the question; first you need to define the term for 1 mark; second you need to make two clear links with the scenario for the other 2 marks.

(b) Identify and outline one defence mechanism and suggest how it might help a person to cope with failing a driving test. **(3 marks)**

⒠ There is a mark for naming a defence mechanism, for example, repression; and another mark for outlining what it means, for example, you might say that repression is motivated forgetting. The third mark is for explaining how the defence mechanism might be used by a person who has failed his/her driving test. A common error in this sort of question is to identify one defence mechanism and then explain a different one. Think before you write the name of the first defence mechanism you can think of. Do you really know what it is and can you link it effectively to the scenario?

(c) Outline two methods that have been used to study cortical specialisation. **(4 marks)**

⒠ This is straightforward. The instruction to outline simply means that you should give a brief description. An extremely brief or slightly inaccurate outline would be worth 1 mark, with 2 marks for an accurate outline that includes correct terminology. If you outline more than two methods the examiner would credit the two best outlines, but you would have wasted precious time. It is much better to think first which two would enable you to offer the most detailed outline.

(d) Describe and evaluate the biological approach in psychology. Refer to evidence in your answer. **(10 marks)**

⒠ Half of the marks are for description and the other half of the marks are for evaluation and analysis. Here you are asked to demonstrate knowledge of the biological approach by offering a clear description, which is probably best done by considering the basic assumptions. Particularly in this area it is important to use the correct terminology to show that you have been studying the topic. The marks for evaluation can be gained by presenting strengths and limitations and using evidence to support what you say. In this question you are asked to 'refer to evidence' in your answer. Remember that if you fail to comply with this instruction, you will be limited to a maximum of 6 marks.

Student A

(a) 'Mediating cognitive' factors is a term used to refer to the thinking that comes between the stimulus and the response. **a** In this case, Sally would have to pay attention to what her mum does and also remember how to do it so she can copy her. **b**

ⓔ **3/3 marks awarded. a** There is a definition and then **b** two good examples of cognitive mediators: paying attention and remembering.

(b) One defence mechanism is displacement. **c** Displacement is where you project your feelings onto something else. In this case, you could slam the door when you get out of the car instead of screaming at the examiner. **d** This would make you feel much better, which is what defence mechanisms do.

ⓔ **2/3 marks awarded. c** Here the student names an appropriate defence mechanism so gets 1 mark, but the definition is not that clear, mainly because of the use of the word 'project' which is not the right word here. In fact, projection is a different defence mechanism altogether. You should note that displacement and projection are often confused by students in exams. **d** The example is a good one and relevant to the situation.

(c) The first method is using scans. A scan is where a machine (PET or MRI) is used to show the parts of the brain that are active when a person is carrying out different activities. Quite often the person is injected with a substance of radioactive properties, which then lights up in a different colour on the scan when that bit of the brain is engaged in a task. **e**

    The second method is EEGs. This is where a person has a lot of electrodes attached to their scalp and each electrode picks up information about levels of brain activity. These are then transmitted to a computer that turns them into waves to be seen on a computer screen. The intensity and frequency of the waves tells us how aroused the person's brain is. **f**

ⓔ **4/4 marks awarded. e** The student correctly outlines scanning techniques. It does not matter that there is no clear distinction between different types of scans and there is enough detail and use of correct terminology here to merit 2 marks for this method. **f** The second method is also sufficiently detailed to be awarded the full 2 marks; there is a description of the basic technique, what equipment is involved and what EEGs show.

(d) The biological approach is one of the most scientific approaches used by psychologists studying behaviour. This is a big strength because it is always important to carry out controlled research and it also makes psychology more respectable as a science. **g**

    One topic of interest for biopsychologists is the study of brain structure, for example showing which parts of the brain are responsible for different abilities and functions. For example, Paul Broca carried out post-mortems and found that language function is controlled by an area on the left frontal lobe called Broca's

area. People with damage to this area have problems producing language. Discoveries like this help psychologists to treat people who have problems and biological therapies such as medication are often used. **h**

Biopsychologists are also involved in studying brain chemicals and hormones. Some interesting hormones are the sex hormones, oestrogen and testosterone. Finding out about how these affect our behaviour is useful to help treat illnesses. **i**

A problem with the biological approach in psychology is that a lot of the research is carried out using animals. As an example, cutting out the hypothalamus in a rat means that it can no longer learn and memorise locations or a route. The findings are then used to try to explain human behaviour. Many people would argue that humans are more complex creatures than other animals and that it is therefore quite wrong to generalise. On the other hand, biological psychologists might feel it is justified because, as Darwin stated, all species are related so we probably have some functions and processes in common with other animals. **j**

🅮 **9/10 marks awarded (AO1 = 5, AO2 = 4).** This answer starts well with a clear statement about the scientific status of the biological approach. **g** The first paragraph is awarded AO1 credit for the point about science and control and evaluation credit for explaining how this has affected the status of psychology. **h** In the second paragraph there is a useful AO1 description of the study of brain structure and function. This is backed up with reference to Broca's research, which is described sufficiently for credit. The final evaluative point is a little bit general but is nevertheless creditworthy. **i** The third paragraph is awarded credit for knowledge of another aspect of the biological approach, but the evaluative point at the end is brief and, in any case, merely a repeat of a previous point. **j** In the final paragraph there is an example of animal research and an extended discussion of the use of animals in psychological research and the issue of generalisation. There is a nice balance here with arguments for and against, which works well. In all, this paragraph is awarded further credit for description and evaluation. As a whole, the answer covers several issues, includes relevant evidence and shows some quite mature and developed evaluation.

Total for this question: 18/20 marks — grade A

Student B

(a) These are cognitive factors that mediate **a** between seeing and copying, so in Sally's case she is watching and mentally noting and is therefore able to do the same. **b**

🅮 **1/3 marks awarded. a** The student attempts to define the term but uses the same terms and therefore cannot get the mark for the definition. **b** As far as the application goes, 1 mark is awarded for 'mentally noting', which is a reference to memory. The reference to 'watching' is behavioural rather than cognitive, so does not get the second mark for application. Perhaps the student means to refer to attention here but it is not clear.

(b) Freud said defence mechanisms help us deal with unpleasant events. **c** There are several defence mechanisms. Rationalisation is a useful one. **d** It helps you to be rational, although if you are upset it is hard to be rational. Here the driver might think that there are already too many cars on the road, so it is really a good thing that hc has failed. **e**

ⓔ **2/3 marks awarded.** **c** This answer starts with a definition of defence mechanisms in general, which is not required. **d** A mark is awarded for rationalisation, although the definition is uninformative and even uses the same term. **e** The example is plausible, however, and is therefore awarded a mark.

(c) Several methods are useful. One common method is the use of scans, which show up bits of the brain that light up when they are active. **f** Another method is the use of an ECG. This is where electrodes are attached to the scalp and the activity can be seen on a screen. **g**

ⓔ **2/4 marks awarded.** **f** This student offers just about enough of an outline of scanning for 1 mark. **g** The second method at first appears as if it will not attract any marks because there is confusion between EEG (use of electrodes to record brain activity) and ECG (use of electrodes to record heart activity). The final sentence has helped the student to achieve 1 mark because there is reference to the scalp, indicating that he/she is discussing brain activity rather than heart activity.

(d) The biological approach is about the study of genes and physical factors that affect behaviour. Twin studies show that lots of behaviours and abilities are related to genetics, and that we inherit them from our parents. Things like intelligence and mental illness etc. could all be genetic in the code of DNA. This code exists in every cell in the body and is called our genotype, which is different to our phenotype, which is genes and environment together. With genes for eye colour you can have a certain genotype for blue eyes but this might not be in the phenotype because your eyes might be brown not showing what you have in your genes. **h**

　　People criticise the biological approach for being too oversimplified. It underplays the role of social influences on behaviour, for example people may become more intelligent because of the way they are treated rather than because of the genes they inherit, but the biological approach does not consider this. **i** Another problem is that it might not be kind to treat people as if they are just biological machines. Biopsychologists use drugs, which can be very helpful to treat illnesses like OCD but is really interfering with nature. **j**

ⓔ **5/10 marks awarded (AO1 = 2, AO2 = 3) h** The first paragraph is awarded AO1 credit for the general point about the focus on genetics and inheritance, and for knowledge of genotypes and DNA. However, the quite protracted elaboration about eye colour adds little. In fact, it rather takes the focus of the answer away from the biological approach in general. There is a lot of other information that might have been included in the description, for example, the role of the brain and nervous system in behaviour, hormones and their effects, and the importance of evolution

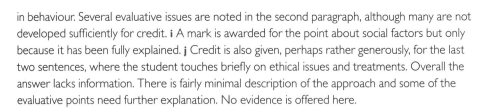

in behaviour. Several evaluative issues are noted in the second paragraph, although many are not developed sufficiently for credit. **i** A mark is awarded for the point about social factors but only because it has been fully explained. **j** Credit is also given, perhaps rather generously, for the last two sentences, where the student touches briefly on ethical issues and treatments. Overall the answer lacks information. There is fairly minimal description of the approach and some of the evaluative points need further explanation. No evidence is offered here.

Total for this question: 10/20 marks — approximately grade D/C

Question 3 **Gender development (I)**

(a) (i) Outline what psychologists mean by *androgyny*.   (2 marks)

(e) This is asking for a clear definition. For 2 marks you are expected to provide some elaboration or detail, e.g. use of additional terminology such as 'masculine' and 'feminine' would be good elaboration here.

(ii) Describe *one* way in which psychologists have studied androgyny.   (2 marks)

(e) This assesses your knowledge of research into androgyny. Note that this is not a full 'Describe a study' question because it is only worth 2 marks. In this question, the focus is simply on the method and not on any one particular study. The most likely answer here will be based on the Bem sex-role inventory. Since there is a lot you could say, it should be relatively easy to give enough detail for 2 marks.

(b) Identify and explain one limitation of the psychodynamic approach to explaining gender development.   (3 marks)

(e) Here you will get 1 mark for identifying a valid limitation. The instruction to 'explain' requires you to elaborate on how or why it is a limitation. When you see the word 'explain' in any question, you should always try to think 'how?' or 'why?' In this question, it is important to remember that you need to think of a limitation that relates to the explanation of gender development and not any old limitation of the psychodynamic approach.

(c) Suggest how a developmental psychologist might investigate gender stability in a child aged 5 years.   (3 marks)

(e) This assesses your understanding of how psychologists carry out research. You need to think what the term 'gender stability' means and then you should be able to recall how gender stability was studied. The wording of the question does allow for any feasible method; so if you can't recall any research into gender stability, but do know what it means, you could propose your own way of studying gender stability. Whether or not this would gain any marks depends on whether what you propose has any face validity. In other words, does the method appear to measure what it is supposed to measure? For the full 3 marks the method must be plausible, must relate to gender stability and must be appropriate for a 5-year-old child.

(d) Discuss nature and nurture in relation to gender development.   (10 marks)

(e) The best way to approach this is to first outline the terms 'nature' and 'nurture', showing that you understand something about the debate. Thereafter this would become a two-sided answer; on the one hand you should present theory and evidence to support the nature side of the argument (the biological explanation for gender and associated research); you should then balance the answer by offering theory and evidence relating to the nurture side of the debate (the social learning explanation for gender and associated research). In this question the AO2 marks for evaluation and analysis are likely to come from appropriate use of evidence, linking it to the key issues in the question, and for comparison of the two sides of the debate. If there is time, you

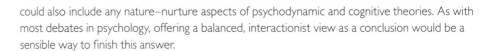

could also include any nature–nurture aspects of psychodynamic and cognitive theories. As with most debates in psychology, offering a balanced, interactionist view as a conclusion would be a sensible way to finish this answer.

Student A

(a) (i) Androgyny means behaving like a man and a woman at the same time, where someone is showing attitudes and abilities of each gender equally. **a**

ⓔ **2/2 marks awarded. a** This answer is not a well-expressed response but the student has the general idea, focusing not just on immediate behaviour but also on more enduring traits.

(ii) Bem studied androgyny using a questionnaire. **b** People had to say which characteristics they were like, and then they got a score for being male and a score for being female at the end. **c** Together this was their androgyny score.

ⓔ **2/2 marks awarded.** This is a basic answer mentioning **b** the questionnaire briefly and **c** the idea that respondents get two scores at the end. There is a lack of detail and some poor expression, but the answer nevertheless conveys the key information about Bem's questionnaire yielding two separate scores.

(b) One problem with the psychodynamic approach to explaining gender is that Freud had no evidence for what he proposed like the Oedipus complex. **d**

ⓔ **1/3 marks awarded. d** The student identifies a valid limitation for 1 mark but there is no further explanation. It is worth noting how the answer is just about related to the development of gender through the reference to the Oedipus complex. Without that there would have been no clear link to gender and the answer would not have gained any marks. There is some opportunity for further marks here. For example, the student could have explained how the Oedipus complex involves an unconscious conflict and that is why it does not lend itself to scientific study.

(c) Gender stability can be studied by asking a child about when they were little. If a child has gender stability they will answer correctly and know that they were always male or female. **e**

ⓔ **1/3 marks awarded. e** The method described here is vague but could just about be seen as a valid way of measuring gender identity, and understanding of the term is implicit.

(d) Over the years many psychologists have said that gender is due to biology. Males and females have different sex chromosomes so it is these that are responsible for gender. In other words, girls are gentle and passive because they do not have a Y chromosome and therefore no testosterone. Males, on the other hand, are aggressive and competitive because they do possess the male Y chromosome and so have testosterone. Injecting animals with testosterone does increase aggression. **f**

    Other psychologists believe that gender is learnt and can be affected by how we are treated. **g** The theory of neutrality (Money) stated that babies in the womb are not either male or female, but will turn out either way because of how they are treated when they are born. To test this, a young boy who had lost his penis in a dreadful accident was brought up as a girl. He was socialised altogether as a girl, given girls' toys to play with, dressed as a girl and also had surgery to make him into a female. **h** However, this study did not end up as the researchers expected because when he reached puberty he decided he did not want to carry on with the treatment and so became a boy again in his behaviour and attitudes. There are many ethical problems with this study. The researchers have been accused of using the boy to test their theory and the consequences were unhappy for him and his family.

Going back to the debate, there is evidence that both nature and nurture are involved in gender, probably in equal measures.

ⓔ **4/10 marks awarded (AO1 = 4, AO2 = 0).** The answer starts without any explicit reference to nature and nurture which is meant to be the focus of the question. Indeed, these terms do not appear at all until the concluding sentence. It is left to the examiner to make links between the content and the question because none are provided by the student. This is not a good strategy because examiners should not have to make the effort for you, and may not give you the benefit of the doubt. Remember to always keep your points focused directly on the question. **f** That said, the first paragraph is awarded credit for knowledge of the biological side (nature) of the debate. The final sentence about injecting animals with testosterone was not creditworthy because there is no obvious link to the question. It could have been made relevant by explaining how such evidence supports the nature side of the debate.

g At the start of the second paragraph the student gets credit for outlining the opposite view, that gender might be learnt, although once again, there is no explicit reference to the debate. **h** The description of the Money study is long-winded and adds little to the answer; however, 1 mark is awarded for a description of a valid study. Had the student explained how the study might be linked to nature or nurture, then more marks would have been awarded. The ethical evaluation of the Money study at the end of the paragraph is wholly irrelevant to this question. The final mention of nature–nurture at the end of the answer is not really sufficient to be awarded any further marks. Notice that this student has not been awarded any of the five AO2 marks available for evaluation or discussion. This could have been addressed quite easily, using little extra material, simply by explaining how the content offered here links to either nature or nurture.

Total for this question: 10/20 marks — approximately grade D/C

Student B

(a) (i) Androgyny refers to a person showing a balanced combination **a** of typically masculine and typically feminine traits and characteristics **b**.

ⓔ **2/2 marks awarded.** This answer gets full marks. **a b** The student expresses the meaning clearly, using appropriate terminology: for example, balance and the terms masculine and feminine.

(ii) Sandra Bem invented the Bem sex-role inventory (BSRI). **c** Respondents have to rate themselves on a scale for 60 adjectives, **d** e.g. shy, forceful etc. Some of the adjectives are typically male and some are typically female. The person's overall masculinity score and femininity score can be calculated at the end, **e** showing whether he/she is androgynous or not.

ⓔ 2/2 marks awarded. c d e This is an excellent answer. It is clearly expressed and includes ample detail of how androgyny has been studied: inventory, rating adjectives, two scores.

(b) According to Freud gender arises in the phallic stage when the child is approximately 4 or 5 years old. This would mean that a child younger than 4 years should not really show any awareness of gender or gender-typed behaviours. **f** However, cognitive psychologists like Kohlberg have shown that children show understanding of gender before the age of 4 years **g** when they have gender identity. These findings suggest that Freud's theory was incorrect.

ⓔ 3/3 marks awarded. g Here the student offers a valid limitation of the psychodynamic approach, which is clearly linked to gender. This shows sound understanding, is well expressed, and **f** includes a full and logical explanation of the problem.

(c) Gender stability comes after gender identity. It is the ability to realise that gender is constant and that we will always be the same gender, and have always been the same in the past. Children get to understand this when about 4 years old, according to Slaby and Frey, who asked children questions like 'When you were a baby, were you a baby girl or a baby boy?' and 'When you grow up will you be a mummy or a daddy?' **h** Depending on the answer, you can tell if they know their gender is the same at all times. For example, if a boy said he used to be a baby girl then he would not show gender stability. **i**

ⓔ 3/3 marks awarded. The answer starts with a definition that shows that the student has a good understanding of what is meant by gender stability. **h** A suitable method is described clearly, the reasoning is sound and **i** the answer is finished off nicely with a sentence explaining how the responses to the questions would relate to gender stability.

(d) Psychologists take different views on the debate about the relative influence of nature and nurture on gender. The extreme nature side would argue that gender is entirely biological, and the extreme nurture side would suggest that gender is entirely due to socialisation as male or female. In reality, it is most likely that both nature and nurture contribute to gender development. **j**

Supporting the nature argument, psychologists have found that biological differences between males and females affect not only physical characteristics, but also gender-related behaviour. **k l** For example, body builders taking male hormones show higher than normal aggression scores on questionnaires. **k** Animal studies, too, support the view that biology (nature) affects gender-related behaviour, **k l** although it is difficult to generalise from animal research to humans **l**. There are similar problems with case study research, e.g. Money's case of Bruce. **k** Such unusual cases seem to show that biology can overrule socialisation, **l** but both are so unusual that they are not that useful to explain normal gender development. **l** It would seem that those who strongly favour the nature side totally disregard the influence of parents and the environment on gender. **m**

This contrasts with the nurture view, **m** which suggests that males and females behave differently because they are reinforced **n** for different types of behaviour. For example, girls are reinforced for behaving gently whilst boys are reinforced for being rough. Studies such as Baby X and Fagot **n** showed that adults and parents do treat male and female infants differently, so supporting the nurture argument. **o** Social learning theory states that people will observe and imitate **n** the behaviour of models; for a young boy the model with whom he closely identifies would be the father, and for a girl, the mother. SLT would therefore support the nurture side of the debate, showing that even if there was no reinforcement, children would inevitably copy the behaviour of a same-sex model. **o**

Cross-cultural studies also explore the influence of nurture. If there are differences in gender behaviour in different cultures, this would suggest that gender is influenced more by nurture, i.e. upbringing and environment, than by biology. **o** Mead's study showed that there are cultural differences, **n** and although she was criticised for being subjective, **o** the same has been found elsewhere.

To conclude the argument, it is inevitable that gender is determined both by nature, in the form of X and Y chromosomes, hormones and brain structure, and by nurture, in the form of social learning through observation and reinforcement. In either case, it seems that gender is determined by internal or external factors and so we do not have free will to choose to behave as either masculine or feminine. **p**

ⓔ 10/10 marks awarded (AO1 = 5, AO2 = 5). j Notice how this student starts by explicitly defining the terms nature and nurture, and then relates them directly to the issue of gender. Having done this at the start, it then makes it much easier for the examiner to see what follows in the context of nature and nurture, and therefore makes it much easier for the student to get marks. **k l** In the second paragraph, the student offers evidence for the nature side of the argument and clearly relates this to the question by using phrases like 'supporting the nature argument' and 'supports the view' . In this way he/she gains **k** AO1 credit for description and knowledge, but also gains **l** AO2 evaluation and analysis credit for the use of evidence. **m** At the end of the nature paragraph, the student gains further evaluation credit for making a contrasting reference relating to the role of parents and environment, which then leads into the next paragraph. In the discussion of social learning and reinforcement, the student makes frequent references back to the issue of nurture and links psychological evidence and theory directly to the question about nurture and gender. Here again, **n** AO1 credit is awarded for knowledge and **o** AO2 credit for use of that knowledge and evidence to answer the question. **p** The final, concluding, paragraph brings together the whole with a neat summary of the interactionist perspective and makes a highly perceptive comment about how both nature and nurture see gender as somehow determined. There is ample content for full marks here. The answer focuses on the question, offers a balance of evidence for each side and links every point sensibly to the question of nature and nurture.

Total for this question: 20/20 marks — grade A

Question 4 Gender development (II)

(a) (i) Identify one androgen.   (1 mark)

ⓔ Here you are required to simply state the name of an androgen (male hormone).

(ii) Briefly describe one method used by psychologists to investigate the influence of androgens on behaviour.   (2 marks)

ⓔ This asks for a brief description. Generally speaking, if 2 marks are on offer then you should try to make two points. Here, for example, 1 mark will be for briefly noting an appropriate method, for example looking at groups with naturally occurring high levels of male hormone, e.g. people with CAH. The second mark will be for describing how this method can be used to tell us anything about the origin of gender-related behaviour.

(b) James is hoping to train as a nurse when he leaves school but his father is trying to persuade him not to. 'Why don't you look at engineering?' says his father hopefully, 'That would be a much better option.'

Explain what is meant by *sex-role stereotyping*. Refer to James in your answer.   (3 marks)

ⓔ Here, 2 of the marks are for defining the term. A good definition would include some mention of 'accepted attitudes/behaviour' or 'expected attitudes/behaviour' and then a reference to males and females. The third mark is for linking the definition to something in the text, for example by commenting on James's father's expectations of his son.

(c) Outline and briefly evaluate one study that supports the social learning explanation for gender development.   (4 marks)

ⓔ This has two distinct elements. To provide a 2-mark outline you need to offer a brief description of a relevant study by noting the method and the findings. The 2-mark discussion part of the question requires you to make some evaluation. You may choose one point and elaborate on it in a couple of sentences, or make two separate points briefly.

(d) Describe and evaluate two cognitive approaches to explaining gender.   (10 marks)

ⓔ Here is a straightforward question with 5 AO1 marks for knowledge of two cognitive approaches (Kohlberg and gender schema theory would be the ones to use) and 5 AO2 marks for evaluation, discussion and comparison. It is important to realise that you must offer two cognitive approaches. If you only cover one, then the maximum marks available would be 6 out of 10. Although the question does not ask for evidence, in 10-mark questions at least 1 mark may be awarded for knowledge of a relevant study, for example Slaby and Frey's gender concept interview or Damon's study of the boy George. Using evidence also allows you to gain AO2 marks by explaining how the evidence supports the theory, or otherwise. Your answer can be structured in two ways. You could cover the two approaches sequentially, describing one approach and evaluating it, then describing the other approach and evaluating it. This is probably the route that most students would prefer. Alternatively, you could integrate descriptions of both the approaches, comparing them and evaluating them as you mention the different aspects. Whichever way you choose to answer, it is possible to access the full 10 marks.

Student A

(a) (i) Testosterone is an androgen. **a**

ⓔ **1/1 mark awarded. a** This gets a mark for identifying testosterone.

(ii) One method is to use female animals. They can be injected with male hormone **b** to see whether it alters their behaviour to be more like that of a male. **c**

ⓔ **2/2 marks awarded. b** There is a clear description of a valid method and **c** an indication of how the outcome would relate to gender-related behaviour.

(b) Sex-role stereotyping is where all members of a particular sex are assumed or expected to be the same. **d** For example, all males are expected to be tough and all females are expected to be gentle. James's father shows sex-role stereotyping by expecting him to be something traditionally male like an engineer. **e**

ⓔ **3/3 marks awarded.** The first sentence offers a reasonable definition which is further clarified by the examples. If an examiner is in any doubt about whether to award a mark or not, it is sometimes useful if the student does offer an example. This might help the examiner to decide between 1 mark or 2 marks. **d** In this case, 2 marks are awarded for the definition with example and **e** 1 mark for the sensible link to the text.

(c) Fagot observed toddlers interacting with parents in their homes. It was found that boys and girls were reinforced and encouraged for different sorts of behaviours. **f** A good thing about this was that it had high ecological validity and so was not artificial. **g**

ⓔ **3/4 marks awarded. f** This answer clearly notes the method and findings of a relevant study. **g** The point about high ecological validity is sensible and just about sufficiently explained for 1 mark. This issue could have been explored in a little more depth if the student had noted how behaviour studied in a natural context is more like normal, everyday behaviour.

(d) One cognitive approach to gender is Kohlberg's theory. He focused on how a child understands gender and thought that gender understanding gets more complex with age and occurs in three stages. The first stage is the gender identity stage where a child around 2 years of age understands what sex he/she is and what sex other people are. The next stage is the gender stability stage where children about 4 years old understand that their gender stays the same in the future. In the final stage of gender constancy, the child of 7 years plus understands that gender stays the same even if outside appearance like clothes or context changes. **h**

Kohlberg's theory describes well and in detail what happens but it doesn't really explain why the child's understanding changes over time. **i** There is evidence to support Kohlberg's theory though. In interviews Slaby and Frey showed that the stages exist **j** when they asked questions to investigate the different stages. **k** For example, a child of 3 years old might not understand that he will remain for ever a boy even though he knows that he is a boy at the moment.

Gender schema theory was proposed by Martin and Halverson. They state that once children realise what they are, male or female, they start to focus on things associated with their own sex and avoid things from the other sex. In this way they build up a schema of 'boy' or 'girl'. This schema then affects how they behave as males or females because the schema is used to guide future behaviour. **l** For example, if a boy knows boys like cars then he will spend more time playing with cars than dolls. Gender schema theory is an improvement on Kohlberg's theory because it explains gender behaviour and not just understanding. **m** It is also a step up from social learning theory because it shows why children imitate models selectively because it fits with their gender schema of what is appropriate for their sex. **n** Despite their great successes, cognitive theories of gender cannot explain gender development on their own. There is probably some biological influence to gender as well. **o**

ⓔ **10/10 marks awarded (AO1 = 5, AO2 = 5).** This is a very good answer, even though there is possibly greater focus on Kohlberg's theory than on gender schema theory. **h** There is a clear description of Kohlberg's theory showing knowledge and understanding of all three stages, which are named correctly, and expressing clearly the basic idea that gender understanding becomes more sophisticated with age. **l** The description of gender schema theory is less detailed but nevertheless accurate and nicely clarified with the use of an example. **k** Although the question does not ask for evidence it is provided here, and would get at least one AO1 mark, although in this case the student has probably done enough elsewhere to achieve the full 5 marks for description. There are a number of relevant evaluative points which gain AO2 credit, **j** for use of evidence where the student links the findings of the study to the theory; **i** the analytical point about the limitation of Kohlberg's theory; **m** comparison between the cognitive theories and **n** comparison with an alternative, namely social learning theory. **o** The final point about cognitive theories in general is also creditworthy.

Total for this question: 19/20 marks — grade A

Student B

(a) (i) Testosterone. **a**

ⓔ **1/1 mark awarded. a** This gets 1 mark.

(ii) One way is to use a correlation method. You could measure the amount or level of testosterone in a person's body and then get a measure of how masculine they are in their behaviour. **b** You would expect a positive correlation **c** if testosterone is linked to masculinity, with high masculinity being linked to high testosterone and vice versa.

ⓔ **2/2 marks awarded.** There is a slight problem with the variable of masculinity because there is no clear idea of how this would be measured but, given that this question is only worth 2 marks, the student has probably done enough here. **b c** The method, measuring the two variables then doing a correlation, is plausible and it is a good answer in the time available.

(b) A sex-role stereotype is where someone should be in a certain role for their sex and so they are being stereotyped. **d** James does not want to be in the stereotype of a male profession because he is keen on a more female-oriented profession. His father is trying to stereotype him into being male. His father has no right to do this.

e **1/3 marks awarded.** This student does not really define the term. Notice how the first sentence, which is meant to be the definition, simply rearranges the words and does not offer anything more. **d** The link to the text does get a mark, however.

(c) The Bandura Bobo doll study showed how children will copy behaviour. In this famous study, children saw an adult behaving aggressively with a doll. Later on, the children copied the model's aggression. This happened more if the model was a boy and the child was also a boy. **e** One problem with this study is that it happened a long time ago. Another problem is the ethics of exposing children to aggression. **f**

e **2/4 marks awarded.** This is a valid study as long as the student focuses on the gender aspect. You probably realise that there were many variations of this study carried out in the 1960s, each with a slightly different aim and method. **e** Here, 1 mark is awarded for the outline because there is a brief reference to gender. There are two brief evaluative points given here. The first is not really explained at all. The student needs to say why it matters that the study took place a long time ago to get any credit. **f** 1 mark is given for the ethical point. Had the student explained how it is important that participants in research are not exposed to harm, then the second mark could have been given.

(d) One cognitive theory of gender is gender schema theory, which states that boys and girls develop a gender schema of what boys are and what girls are. **g** In the stage theory it is stated that children develop a gender schema for their own gender first and then the other gender later. **h** Another theory is Kohlberg's. His is also a stage theory but he doesn't say anything about understanding own gender first and other gender afterwards, **i** although, of course, that could be the case. According to Kohlberg we can label ourselves first and can point to a photo of a boy or girl when asked. This is labelling. Later on we know that our gender has consistency and will be the same no matter what. The other stage is the stability stage where ideas remain stable for ever. **j**

Alternatives to cognitive theory are the biological and social learning theory. Biologists assume that gender is all down to genes and chromosomes, and social learning theory believes that gender is learnt by watching other people like models and copying them. This was demonstrated in the Bobo doll study by Bandura.

e **4/10 marks awarded (AO1 = 3, AO2 = 1).** **h** The student makes one creditworthy point about gender schema theory with the reference to development of own-sex schema before other-sex schema. **g** The general point about what a gender schema contains is also worth credit.

j The description of Kohlberg is rather confused and inaccurate, but perhaps worthy of some AO1 credit. **i** There is a half-hearted comparison between gender schema theory and Kohlberg that is just about worth AO2 credit. The alternative theories are simply tagged on at the end without any attempt to compare them with cognitive theories. As such, this last paragraph is completely redundant and gets no credit at all. Always be careful when you present alternative theories as part of a discussion. These will only count if you make clear links between them and the theory under discussion. Stand alone alternatives, like the ones here, are worth nothing because they are not being used to answer the question.

Total for this question: 10/20 marks — approximately grade D/C

Question 5 **Research methods (I)**

A biopsychologist investigating reaction time to different stimuli decides to carry out an experiment with two conditions. He recruits participants from the college canteen, asking anyone who is around to take part. He tells them that it is a 'fun experiment' and that he will explain it all to them afterwards.

In one condition, participants have to press a button on a computer as soon as they hear a noise through headphones they are wearing. In the other condition, the same participants, again wearing headphones, have to press the button as soon as they see a coloured light appear in the centre of the computer screen. Half of the participants perform in the light condition first and the noise condition second. For the other half of the participants the conditions are in the opposite order.

For each condition, the psychologist records the individual response times on five separate trials, and then takes the average response time for each participant. These averages are then used to calculate an overall average response time for each condition.

At the end of the study, when the psychologist debriefs the participants, one of them is upset when told that his reaction time of 200 milliseconds in the light condition is much higher than that of all the other participants.

Mean response time (in milliseconds) for the noise stimulus condition and the light stimulus condition

	Noise stimulus condition	Light stimulus condition
Mean response time (milliseconds)	80	60

(a) Sketch a bar graph that could be used to display the mean response times. Label and title your graph.
(3 marks)

ⓔ This asks for a sketch. There will probably be a section of graph paper in your answer book. Out of the 3 marks, I mark is for a title which should include the units of measurement (e.g. milliseconds) and the names of both conditions, I mark is for axis labels on the x- and y-axes, and the third mark is for plotting the graph.

(b) The researcher uses the mean time in milliseconds as a measure of central tendency. Explain one problem of using the mean in this study.
(2 marks)

ⓔ You are asked to link your answer to this study. This wording is often used in the research methods questions and means that you cannot offer any old problem (in this case with the use of the mean), but must gear your answer specifically to the study described.

(c) Name the experimental design the researcher used in this experiment.
(1 mark)

ⓔ Here you are simply asked to name the experimental design so there is no need to write a sentence if you know the name. If you don't know the exact name for the design, but could try to describe it, then you might get a mark for that. It is worth a go.

(d) Explain why it was necessary for the order of conditions to be reversed for half of the participants. What is the name of this technique? (3 marks)

This requires a named technique associated with the experimental design used for the study. As in the previous question, it is worth describing the technique if you don't know the name for it, as you might get a mark. The other 2 marks are for explaining why the technique was used. Again, it would be sensible to link your answer to the study being described.

(e) Explain why it was important for the participants to wear the headphones in both conditions of the experiment. (2 marks)

This is a question about control of extraneous variables and you would need to say this for full marks. However, even someone who did not use the correct terminology might be able to offer a reasonable common-sense explanation. A word of advice here: in the research methods section there are often questions that can be answered reasonably correctly by using common-sense. Never leave a gap, even if you are not sure, as you could be lucky.

(f) Explain *one* ethical problem involved in this study and suggest how it might have been avoided. (3 marks)

Here your knowledge of ethical issues is tested. Several answers could be appropriate, although one particular issue stands out in the description of the study. Always try to use the BPS terminology when you refer to ethical issues. Note that this sub-section of the question is really in two parts, explanation and suggestion, and you must address both aspects to get full credit.

(g) The researcher decided to carry out an unstructured interview with the participant who had a very high reaction time in the light condition.

(i) Explain what is meant by an *unstructured interview*. (2 marks)

This is a straightforward question about unstructured interviews, although remember to elaborate sufficiently for 2 marks.

(ii) Suggest one reason why an unstructured interview might be useful in this situation. (1 mark)

You are asked to link what you know about unstructured interviews to the situation described in the text. Remember there is only 1 mark available here so you will only get 1 mark even if you offer more than one reason. If you do offer more than one, then the examiner will credit you for any one that is correct, but you will have wasted time that might have been better spent elsewhere.

(h) The researcher obtained participants from the college canteen.

(i) Identify the sampling technique used in this investigation. (1 mark)

You are simply asked to identify the sampling technique. If you know the correct term then a sentence is not necessary.

AQA(B) AS Psychology

(ii) Suggest *one* strength and *one* limitation of this sampling technique.   (2 marks)

ⓔ There is only 1 mark each for the strength and the limitation so you can make your answers quite brief.

Student A

(a) Bar graph to show the mean response times for the two conditions.

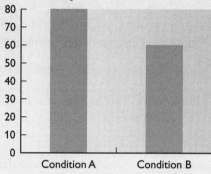

ⓔ **1/3 marks awarded. a** The graph is correctly plotted, but this student does not give a full title and the axis labels are incomplete/incorrect.

(b) The mean is found by adding together all the scores and then dividing by the number of scores. **b** It is a very sensitive measure of average. **c** One problem is that the mean is quite difficult to calculate if there are a lot of scores. **d**

ⓔ **0/2 marks awarded. b** This student starts by explaining how the mean is calculated, even though the question does not ask for that information. Many students waste time doing this and get no marks for it. **c** In this case it is made worse as the student gives an advantage of using the mean, which is not asked for either. **d** When he/she finally gets around to answering the question, he/she makes the mistake of giving a general point and not relating it to this study. In fact, we are not told how many participants there are altogether so it may not be the case that 'there are lots of scores'. The correct answer here requires reference to the problem of using the mean where there are one or two very high or low scores. No marks for this part of the question.

(c) This is a repeated measures design **e** with the same people in each condition.

ⓔ **1/1 mark awarded. e** The mark is given here for correctly identifying the design.

(d) This is so that they don't all do better in the second condition because they have already had a go at the reaction time task and know what to expect. **f**

ⓔ **1/3 marks awarded. f** The mark here is for noting the possibility of a practice effect (although this term is not used). There is no further explanation of the concept of order effects, nor is there any reference to the name of the technique (counterbalancing).

(e) This is so that the researcher can be sure that the times are not different because of the headphones rather than because of the type of stimulus. **g**

🄔 **1/2 marks awarded. g** The student correctly explains the importance of controlling for extraneous variables, although neither the term 'control' nor the term 'extraneous variables' is used in the answer. This is a good example of a common-sense answer.

(f) One ethical problem would be the upset caused to those participants who do not do very well. People should not be distressed or feel different about themselves because of what has happened in an experiment. **h** This could have been avoided by sensitive handling. **i**

🄔 **2/3 marks awarded. h** Marks are awarded for an explanation of the issue although there is no use of BPS terminology. **i** The student's attempt to address the second part of the question is a little vague and not worth a mark.

(g) (i) This is where there are no questions set beforehand and everyone has different questions. **j**

🄔 **2/2 marks awarded. j** This would have been a much better answer if there had been reference to how an unstructured interview starts with a general aim, or if the student had offered some expansion of the 'different questions' point.

(ii) It would be useful because you can find out things that the experiment maybe did not show: for example, if the person had a high reaction time for a reason. **k**

🄔 **1/1 mark awarded. k** This suggestion is appropriate, relevant to the study in question and therefore worth a mark.

(h) (i) This is opportunity sampling. **l**

🄔 **1/1 mark awarded. l** A mark is awarded here.

(ii) One strength is that it is cheap. **m** One limitation is that it would usually be applied to a limited range of people, so cannot be used to generalise the results. **n**

🄔 **1/2 marks awarded. m** Students often refer to opportunity sampling as a 'cheap' method and it never gets any marks. **n** The limitation is valid and gains a mark.

Total for this question: 11/20 marks — approximately grade C/D

Student B

(a) Bar graph to show the mean response times in milliseconds in the light stimulus and noise stimulus conditions. **a**

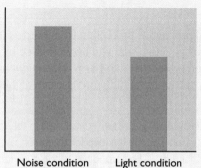

⊜ 2/3 marks awarded. a The title gets a mark as it includes the units of measurement (milliseconds) and has the two named conditions (noise and light). **b** The axis labels are correct for another mark. Although the plotting looks to be approximately correct, there are no units on the y-axis, which are required to get the third mark.

(b) In this study there is an extreme score (the person with the very high reaction time). This extreme score will distort the mean and make it higher than it really should be, making the mean less representative of the scores as a whole. **c**

⊜ 2/2 marks awarded. c Marks here for a correctly identified problem that relates directly to this study.

(c) Repeated measures design. **d**

⊜ 1/1 mark awarded. d 1 mark for identifying the experimental design.

(d) This is counterbalancing. It is necessary to control for the effects of order where participants perform in each condition. Performance in the second condition may be better because participants have had a practice, or it may be worse because they are tired (fatigue effect). **e**

⊜ 3/3 marks awarded. e This is a good 3-mark answer that includes a full explanation of the concept of order effects and names the technique correctly.

(e) This is to control for an extraneous variable and is to ensure that any difference in performance is not simply due to the wearing of headphones rather than the type of stimulus being responded to. **f**

(e) **2/2 marks awarded. f** This answer correctly identifies the issue using the appropriate terminology. Contrast this with the answer given by student A. Both students are aware of the key issue, but this answer shows evidence of study in the correct use of important methodological terminology.

> **(f)** One ethical problem is protection from harm. **g** The person who has a very high score in the light condition will be distressed by taking part in the study and so has not been protected from harm. This might have been avoided simply by not telling him outright that his score is much higher than everyone else's scores. **h**

(e) **3/3 marks awarded. g** The key ethical issue in the study is identified using the BPS terminology for 1 mark. This is expanded for the second mark in a description of just how the person might be affected. **h** The second half of the question is sensibly addressed for the third mark.

> **(g) (i)** This is where there is a general aim in mind but no pre-determined questions. The researcher prompts the interviewee and can ask extra questions as issues arise. **i**

(e) **2/2 marks awarded. i** This is a good answer that includes reference to the aim instead of pre-set questions and the possibility of the questions being specific to the interviewee.

> **(ii)** It might be useful to find out a reason why this person had a much higher score than other people, for example, perhaps he/she normally wears glasses but was not wearing glasses during the experiment. **j**

(e) **1/1 mark awarded. j** This is a sensible response linked directly to the study described in the question.

> **(h) (i)** This is opportunity sampling. **k**

(e) **1/1 mark awarded. k** A mark is awarded.

> **(ii)** This is a very quick method as you do not have to look out especially for people with particular characteristics. **l** Bias is a problem though, because the researcher is choosing whoever he wants. **m**

(e) **2/2 marks awarded. l** 1 mark is awarded for the strength and **m** 1 mark for the limitation. Notice there is evidence that the student understands both the issues. Had the student simply said that this method of sampling is 'quick' but possibly 'biased', the marks could not be awarded quite so confidently. Assertions like this should always be explained to be sure of credit.

Total for this question: 19/20 marks — grade A

Question 6 **Research methods (II)**

A team of psychologists set out to investigate the attitudes of university students towards healthy eating. They expect students on health-related courses to have a more positive attitude to healthy eating than students on other courses. They recruit a stratified sample of 200 university students from one university. They measure attitudes using a questionnaire about food preferences. The questionnaires are scored to give an overall 'preference for healthy food' score for each participant.

(a) Write a suitable hypothesis for this investigation.   (2 marks)

Here a full-mark hypothesis should include both conditions of the independent variable and also the dependent variable. These should be clearly stated and operationalised. Although the text points to a difference in a specific direction, at this level it does not matter whether you provide a directional hypothesis or simply predict a difference. Although knowledge of null hypotheses is not required, a null hypothesis could also gain 2 marks here.

(b) Write an open question that could be used in the questionnaire.   (1 mark)

This question must allow respondents to put any answer they like. Be careful not to use questions where the only sensible answer could be 'yes' or 'no'.

(c) Write a closed question that could be used in the questionnaire.   (1 mark)

The question should have a fixed number of optional answers, which you need to specify. Note that the questions for both (b) and (c) must be about food preferences to gain credit.

(d) Identify *one* strength and *one* limitation of using open questions.   (2 marks)

Here the examiner is expecting a brief answer, as you are asked simply to 'identify'. You do not need to use long sentences and could answer in note form to save time. You must, however, indicate clearly which is the strength and which is the limitation.

(e) Explain how the psychologists might have selected a stratified sample of students from the university.   (3 marks)

This is worth 3 marks so you will need to offer some detail. Notice that this question is not asking you to define a stratified sample, but is asking how you would go about selecting a stratified sample from the population of students at one university.

When the questionnaire data are analysed, the psychologists find that students are dissatisfied with the food at one of the university catering facilities. They decide to carry out a covert observation at this facility to observe students' behaviour. They are interested in whether students just eat there, or whether they use the facility for other purposes. They draw up a record chart for their observation.

(f) **Explain what is meant by** *covert observation* **and suggest** *one* **reason why psychologists might prefer to use a covert observation.** (2 marks)

  ⓔ Here you get 1 mark for saying briefly what the term means, and the other mark for explaining why covert observations might be preferred.

(g) **Draw a suitable record chart that the psychologists could use for their observation showing at least** *two* **categories of behaviour.** (3 marks)

  ⓔ 1 mark is for the construction of some form of tally chart. The other 2 marks are for relevant categories of observable behaviours that might occur when the students use the catering facility.

(h) **Identify and explain** *one* **ethical issue involved in this observation.** (3 marks)

  ⓔ You are expected to identify a relevant ethical issue for the first mark. You should use the terminology from the BPS code of conduct here. The other 2 marks are for the explanation, which you should link to the study being considered here. In your explanation you could say why this particular ethical issue matters and why or how it should be taken into consideration.

(i) **In this case the psychologists carried out their observation in a natural setting. Briefly discuss the use of natural observations.** (3 marks)

  ⓔ You will need to comment on the use of natural observations. There are various ways you could get the marks here. You could outline strengths and/or limitations of natural observations; or you could compare natural observations with the alternative, controlled observations.

> **Student A**
>
> **(a)** Students on health courses have more positive attitudes to healthy food. **a**

  ⓔ **1/2 marks awarded. a** This is an incomplete hypothesis but is along the right lines.

> **(b)** How often do you eat fresh vegetables in a week? **b**

  ⓔ **1/1 mark awarded. b** This is a valid example of an open question that is relevant to the topic.

> **(c)** Are you healthy? Yes/No **c**

  ⓔ **0/1 mark awarded. c** Although this is a closed question, it is not actually about food preferences.

> **(d)** Strength — any answer will do, which is good. Limitation — people might not be able to think of anything to put down. **d**

ⓔ **0/2 marks awarded. d** Neither the strength nor the limitation is good enough to be awarded a mark.

> **(e)** A stratified sample means there are different groups like students from different courses. Some would be language students etc. **e**

ⓔ **1/3 marks awarded. e** A mark is awarded here because the student seems to have some understanding of the importance of sub-groups in a stratified sample.

> **(f)** A covert observation is an undercover observation where no one can see the observer. This is better as people do not act up or show off in front of the observer. **f**

ⓔ **2/2 marks awarded. f** Although not very well expressed, this is good enough.

> **(g)** Record chart: **g**

Chatting with friend	Alone reading	In large group

ⓔ **3/3 marks awarded. g** The record chart is suitable and has at least two valid categories.

> **(h)** One ethical issue is asking consent. **h** If you do not make the observer obvious, it means that people have not given their consent and cannot withdraw if they wish. **i**

ⓔ **2/3 marks awarded. h** The issue of consent is a valid one and **i** the student extends this a little by pointing out how one consequence of not gaining consent means that the participants cannot choose to withdraw from the study at any time. These two issues might be seen as separate ethical points, but they do overlap, so marks are gained here.

> **(i)** A strength is that behaviour will be more normal and not artificial. **j**

ⓔ **1/3 marks awarded. j** For further marks the examiner would expect to see some elaboration, for example, an explanation of how or why behaviour would be 'more normal'.

Total for this question: 11/20 marks — approximately grade C

(a) Students on health-related courses will get a higher score on the questionnaire than students on non-health courses. **a**

ⓔ **2/2 marks awarded. a** This is a good hypothesis with both conditions of the IV specified (types of course, i.e. health-related and non-health-related) and a clear DV (score on the questionnaire).

(b) b Which five foods do you like best?

ⓔ **1/1 mark awarded. b** This is a nice open question.

(c) Which of these do you eat at least once a week? (Tick which foods apply): **c**

Vegetables	Lean meat/fish	Beans/pulses	Whole cereals

ⓔ **1/1 mark awarded. c** This is a good closed question.

(d) One strength is that the responses are more likely to be valid as people can be quite truthful and say their real answer. **d** The problem is in analysis as there are no categories so it is difficult to see patterns and do graphs. **e**

ⓔ **2/2 marks awarded. d e** Both the strength and the limitation are valid.

(e) They would need participants from different groups in the population. They could divide up the students according to year or type of course. Then they need to select from each group in ratio according to how many there are for each group in the population. So, if there are more students in Year 1, then there should be more in the sample from Year 1. The final selection should be randomly done. **f**

ⓔ **3/3 marks awarded. f** The student has correctly noted the key issues involved in stratified sampling: identification of sub-groups, representation in proportion, random selection from each sub-group.

(f) This is where the observer cannot be seen by those being observed. This helps to ensure that the behaviour being observed is more natural. **g**

ⓔ **2/2 marks awarded. g** Both elements are here so this answer gets both marks.

(g) Record chart to record frequencies of observed behaviours. **h**

	Eating	Reading
Frequency tally		

ⓔ **3/3 marks awarded. h** The record chart is suitable and has two valid categories.

(h) A key issue is informed consent. Ideally participants should give consent and know what they are consenting to. However, in this study it would make the observation pointless. The BPS code states that privacy should not be infringed and that observations are alright if carried out in a public place, such as the canteen, because people would normally expect to be observed there. In this case there is no need to ask for consent because they are in a public place. **i**

ⓔ **3/3 marks awarded. i** The issues of consent and privacy are both relevant and each of these alone could have formed the basis of an answer. Here they are rather cleverly linked so all the content is deemed relevant and the answer is therefore fully elaborated.

(i) This means that the results have greater validity. The behaviour is more true to life because the study takes place in a real-life context. **j** This is better than controlled observations where you are less likely to see true behaviours because they are occurring out of their usual context. **k**

ⓔ **3/3 marks awarded. j** Although the issue is the same as that expressed by the previous student, this answer is rather more impressive because the student uses the correct terminology, referring to 'context' and 'validity'. **k** He/she has followed the instruction to discuss by presenting some comparison with the alternative type of observation.

Total for this question: 20/20 marks — grade A

Knowledge check answers

1 The four main influences are genes, biological structures, brain chemistry and evolution.

2 Biological determinism means that behaviour is controlled/governed by our biological make-up.

3 Reflex or involuntary behaviours can be learned through classical conditioning.

4 Operant conditioning can explain how we learn a wide range of voluntary behaviours, not just reflexes.

5 Mediating cognitive factors are mental processes, such as memory, that occur between stimulus and response.

6 A model is a structured theory representing a mental process, usually involving a sequence of stages.

7 Research methods used are laboratory experiments, case studies, computer modelling and scans.

8 According to Freud, the unconscious motivates all our behaviour.

9 Example: a mother might only love her daughter if she gets good A-level grades.

10 Examples of neurons: motor — carry messages from the brain to the muscles; sensory — carry messages from the senses to the brain; inter — send messages from neurons to other neurons.

11 It controls basic involuntary functions, and is sub-divided into the sympathetic and parasympathetic sections.

12 The areas are (i) Broca's area and (ii) Wernicke's area.

13 The methods are scans, EEGs and post-mortems.

14 The chemical messengers are neurotransmitters.

15 Adrenalin is produced in the adrenal gland, and causes bodily arousal, speeding up bodily responses as in the fight or flight response.

16 Sex is biological, gender comprises the social roles, attitudes and behaviours associated with each sex — being masculine or feminine; sex is fixed, gender can change.

17 The debate is about the extent to which biological and environmental influences affect gender.

18 They study these to see whether sex chromosomes affect gender-related behaviour.

19 Testosterone — aggression; oestrogen — emotional outbursts.

20 With imitation we can copy anyone; with identification, it has to be a specific person to whom we feel some attachment or admiration.

21 Identity Q: 'Are you a boy or a girl?'; stability Q: 'When you grow up will you be a mummy or a daddy?'; constancy Q: (to a boy) 'If you put on a dress will you still be a boy?'

22 A gender schema is a unit of knowledge about behaviours and roles appropriate for males/females.

23 Freud stated identification must be with same-sex parent in the phallic stage; for SL theorists, identification can be with anyone at any time.

24 The aim is general whereas the hypothesis is very specific and testable.

25 The stratified technique.

26 The laboratory experiment.

27 They should use counterbalancing.

28 They should use random allocation to conditions.

29 The unstructured interview.

30 Observers record the behaviour that they see rather than their opinion.

31 This is because there are no participants being studied directly.

32 Mean = 4.5; median = 3.5; mode = 2.

33 Range = 12.

34 The standard deviation (SD) is much more sensitive than the range because it takes all the scores into account.

35 A code of ethics protects participants, maintains standards and provides guidelines for psychologists.

AQA(B) AS Psychology

A

acetylcholine (ACH) 14
action potential 14
adrenal glands 18
adrenalin 18
aggression 23
aims 29
alternative hypothesis 30
androgens 23, 62, 63
androgyny **20**, 57, 58, 59–60
approaches
    biopsychology 6–7, 13–18
    key approaches 6–13
    summary 19
appropriateness, and
    imitation 25
assessment objectives 46
autism **7**
autonomic nervous
    system 15, 17–18
axons 14

B

Bandura, A. 9, 25
bar charts 40, 67, 69, 71
behaviourism 7–9, 47,
    48–49, 50
Bem's sex-role inventory
    (BSRI) 20
bias 30, 32, 37, 38
biological determinism 7
biopsychology 6–7, 13–18,
    22–24
    exam questions 47, 48,
        52, 53–54, 55
brain, localisation of
    function 15–17, 52, 53, 55
brain plasticity 16
brain structure, and gender 23
British Psychological
    Society 42
Broca's area 16, 17

C

case studies 7, 10, 12, 13, 38
category systems 37, 38, 74,
    75, 77
cause-and-effect
    relationships 34, 36
cell body 14
central nervous system **15**
central tendency **39**, see
    also mean

childhood experiences 11
Chodorow, N. 28
chromosomes 6, 22–23
classical conditioning **8**, 48
client-centred therapy 13
closed questions 34, 73, 74, 76
code of ethics 42
cognitive approach 10–11,
    25–27
    exam questions 47, 48,
        49, 62, 63–64, 65–66
cognitive developmental
    theory 25–26
cognitive factors (mediating)
    9, 25, 52, 53, 54
competence 42
computer analogy 10
computerised axial
    tomography (CAT) 17
conditioning 8, 48–49, 50
conditions of worth **13**,
    47–48, 49
confidentiality 42
confounding variables 32
congenital adrenal
    hyperplasia (CAH) 23
consent 42, 77
content analysis 37–38
continuous recordings 37
controlled observation 36
corpus callosum 15
correlation studies 35–36, 41
cortical specialisation
    16–17, 52, 53, 55
cortisol 18
counterbalancing 33, 71
covert observation 37,
    73–74, 75, 76–77
cultural variation 21

D

Damon, W. 26
data representation 40–41,
    67, 69, 71
debriefs 42
deception 42
defence mechanisms 11, 12,
    52, 53, 55
demand characteristics 34
dendrites 14
dependent variable
    (DV) **31**, 32, 40

descriptive statistics 39
discrimination 8
dispersion **39**
DNA 14, see also genetics
dopamine 14
double-blind research 32

E

ecological validity 10, **11**,
    25, 31, 34
ego 11
Ehrhardt, A. 22
Electra complex 27
electroencephalograms
    (EEGs) **17**
endocrine system **18**
environmental determinism 9
Erikson, E. 28
ethics 7, 34, 37, 38, 42
    exam questions 68, 70,
        72, 74, 75, 77
evolution 6
examinations
    assessment objectives 46
    question types 44–46
    sample questions 44, 47–77
experimental designs
    33–34, 67, 69, 71
experimental hypothesis 30
experimental methods 7,
    10, 31–34, 36
experimenter bias 32
extinction 8
extraneous variables **32**,
    36, 68, 70, 71–72

F

Fagot, B. 24
fatigue effect 33
femininity 20
field experiments 31
fixation **11**
free will 12
frequencies 40
Freud, S. 11, 27
Frey, K. S. 26

G

gender 19
gender constancy 25, 26
gender development
    concepts 19–21
    exam questions 57–66

explaining 21–28
    summary 28–29
gender identity 25, 26
gender schema
    theory 26–27
gender (sex role) stereotypes
    20–21, 62, 63, 65
gender stability 25, 26, 57,
    58, 60
generalisation
    and conditioning 8
    of findings 6, 7, 9, 13
genes 6
genetics 14, 22–23, 47, 48,
    49, 55
genotype **6**, 47, 48, 49, 55
graphical displays 40–41,
    67, 69, 71

H

Halverson, C. 26
hemispheric
    specialisation 15–16
hierarchy of needs 13
hormones 18, 23, 62, 63, 64
Horney, K. 28
humanistic approach 12–13,
    47–48
hypothalamus 18, 23
hypotheses 30, 73, 74, 76

I

id 11
identification 9, 24, 27
imitation 9, 24, 25
Imperato McGinley, J. 22
incongruence 12
independent groups
    design 33
independent variable (IV) **31**,
    32, 40
informed consent 42, 77
integrity 42
interactionism 21
internal mental processes
    10, 47, 48, 49
interneurons 14
inter-observer reliability 37
interviews 35, 68, 70, 72

K

Katz, P.A. 20
Klinefelter's syndrome 22
Kohlberg, L. 25

L

laboratory experiments 7, 10, 31
language 16
lateralisation of function 15–16
line graphs 40–41
Lloyd, B. B. 24
localisation of brain function 15–17, 52, 53, 55
long-answer questions 45

M

magnetic resonance imaging (MRI) 17
Martin, C. 26
masculinity 20
matched pairs design 33–34
Mead, M. 21
mean 39, 67, 69
median 39
mediating cognitive factors 9, 25, 52, 53, 54
memory 10, 48, 49
mode 39
modelling 9, 24, 25
models 10, 48
Money, J. 22
motor neurons 14
multi-store model of memory 10
myelin sheath 14

N

natural observation 36, 74, 75, 77
nature-nurture debate 21, 57–59, 60–61
neo-Freudian theory **28**
nervous system 15–18
neurons 14
neurotransmitters **14**
non-experimental methods 34–38
non-participant observation 36

O

objectivity 7, 34, 36
observation 9, 10, 36–37, 73–74, 75, 76–77
observer bias 37
observer effect 36–37
Oedipus complex 27, 28

oestrogen 23
open questions 35, 73, 74, 76
operant conditioning 8, 50
operationalisation 30
opportunity samples 30
oral stage 11
order effects 33, 71
overt observation 36–37

P

parasympathetic system 15, 17–18
participant observation 36
Pavlov, I. 8
penis envy 27, 28
peripheral nervous system 15, 17
phallic stage 27
phenomenology 13
phenotype **6**, 47, 48, 49, 55
phenylketonuria (PKU) 6
pilot studies **38**
pituitary gland 18
planning, of research 29–31
populations 30–31
positron-emission tomography (PET) 17
post-mortems **17**
practice effect 33, 68, 69, 71
pre-menstrual syndrome (PMS) 23
primacy-recency effect 10
privacy 42
protection 42
psychoanalysis 12
psychoanalytic theory 27–28
psychodynamic approach 11–12, 27–28, 57, 58, 60
psychosexual stages 11, 27
punishment 8

Q

Q-sort 13
qualitative research 29
quantitative research 29
quasi-experiments 32
questionnaires 34, 38, 73, 74, 76
questions *see* examinations, research questions

R

random allocation 33
random samples 30

range 39
Raynor, R. 8
recording techniques 37
reductionism 7
reinforcement **8**, **9**, 24
reliability 34, 37
repeated (related) measures design 33
replication **34**
representativeness 30, 31
researcher bias 30, 38, *see also* experimenter bias, observer bias
research hypotheses 30
research methods
  and approaches 7, 9, 10, 12, 13, 17, 52, 53, 55
  descriptive statistics 39
  ethics 42
  exam questions 46, 67–77
  experimental 31–34
  non-experimental 34–38
  planning research 29–31
  representing data 40–41
  summary 43
research questions 29–30
respect 42
responsibility 42
Rogers, C. 12

S

samples **30**, 73, 75, 76
sampling 30–31, 68–69, 70, 72
sampling bias 30
scans 7, 10, 17
scattergrams 35, 36, 41
scenario questions 45
scientific approaches 7, 9, 11
  rejection of 12, 13
Seavey, C. A. 20
self 12
self-actualisation **13**
self-report methods 34–35, *see also* interviews, questionnaires
sensory neurons 14
serotonin 14
sex 19
sex chromosomes 22–23
sex-role stereotypes 20–21, 62, 63, 65
sexually dimorphic nucleus **23**

short answer questions 44–45
similarity, and imitation 25
Skinner, B. F. 8
Slaby, R. G. 26
Smith, C. 24
social construction of gender 19
social learning theory 9–10, 24–25, 52, 62, 63, 65
somatic nervous system 15
standard deviation (SD) 39
standardised instructions 32, 38
statistics 39
stratified samples 30–31, 73, 75, 76
structured interviews 35
subjectivity **34**
summary tables 40
superego 11
sympathetic system 15, 17–18
synapse 14
synaptic transmission 14
systematic samples 31

T

tabular displays 40
target populations 30
terminal button 14
testosterone 23
therapies 11, 12, 13
time sampling 37
token economy systems 9
Turner's syndrome 22
twin studies 7

U

unconscious 11
unstructured interviews 35, 68, 70, 72
Urberg, K. A. 20–21

V

validity 34, 35, 36, 38
vesicles 14
vicarious reinforcement **9**, 24

W

Watson, J. B. 8
Wernicke's area 16
withdrawal from research 42

Z

Zalk, S. R. 20

AQA(B) AS Psychology